the**IU**

THE INTERNATIONAL UNION
FOR LAND VALUE TAXATION

The Marginalists and the Special Status of Land as a Factor of Production

Herman-Heinrich Gossen, Friedrich von Wieser, León Walras, and Wilfredo Pareto – Resemblances and differences with Henry George

FERNANDO SCORNIK GERSTEIN

&

FRED E. FOLDVARY

Published in the UK in 2010 by
The International Union for Land Value Taxation and Free Trade
Studio 5, St. Oswald's Studio
Sedlescombe Road
London SW6 1RH
www.theIU.org

First published 2010

isbn 978-0-904658-11-8

Typesetting and design by Motherlode.

The authors are responsible for any errors and for the views
expressed in this study.

Contents

i. Preface

This is a fascinating and insightful study of how the radical egalitarian views of three beautiful minds were bowdlerlzed by homelier minds and passed forward to modern students as complacent rationalizations of the status quo. These three were the continental Europeans Hermann-Heinrich Gossen, Friedrich von Wieser, and Léon Walras. To them the authors add the fascistic mind of Vilfredo Pareto, and how this last is what shaped the modern economic canon. The Anglophonic clerisy, beholden to geocratic patrons, beatified Pareto and overlooked his fascism because his ideas helped them merge land with capital goods and thus stymie the most dangerous challenge to the ruling classes. This challenge was not Marxism, not in America or Britain, but the one posed by Henry George and like-minded activists in the Populist-Progressive Era in America. Under other names this movement had counterparts in most advanced and developing nations in the same period.

Desk-bound scholars will also value new translations of fragments, at least, from Spanish, French, German, Italian and even Russian sources: a pancontinental smorgasbord of economic thought.

Hermann-Heinrich Gossen was, like the better known Ernst Engel (of "Engel's Law"), a Prussian bureaucrat. Writing in 1854 Gossen developed the equimarginal principle. Others neglected his ideas almost entirely until Jevons unearthed them in 1879 – but only to praise his mathematics and his conceptual insights, not the controversial part of his work that caused it to be so neglected. This was his proposal to nationalize land.

Gossen's proposal did not cause him to be imprisoned or shot because its implementation was to be less drastic than it sounds. The state was not to administer enterprises on its lands, but make them available to private enterprise by leasing them out – much as the U.S.A. leases out parts of its vast remaining public domain today, only better and more efficiently. He would compensate present owners. His thinking was that the state could do this and profit because of its better credit rating and longer time-horizon. Later writers Walras and Alfred Russel Wallace advanced the same idea – and met the same oblivion. What we know of prodigal states today makes one doubt the realism of the postulate, but it was a tribute to the Prussian administration of his day that he could entertain such a thought. To demonstrate the point Gossen worked out the mathematics of discounting cash flows under conditions of rising rents. His mathematical skill was also a tribute to the numeracy of German education, for German forest economists, notably Martin Faustmann, were at the same time pioneering the use of mathematics in forest valuation and management.

Friedrich von Wieser was a pioneer of the "Austrian" school, of thought. Unlike Menger and Bőhm-Bawerk, Wieser har-

The Marginalists and the Special Status of Land as a Factor of Production

bored egalitarian thoughts based on the idea of diminishing marginal utility. He wrote specifically about taxing urban land rents. Scornik Gerstein and Foldvary note that modern leaders and exemplars of the Austrian school neglect Wieser relative to its other pioneers. This writer notes with regret – and without knowing if the authors of this work will agree - that the moderns make "Austrian" almost synonymous with "libertarian". Presumably the recent debacle led by Greenspan and other libertarians in Washington will force some rethinking of this policy, but like other intellectual changes it will take time while the world will move on ahead of it.

Walras found himself unemployable in his native France because of his ideas on nationalizing land. He found refuge at Lausanne, in Switzerland, over heavy opposition, so he and his ideas are identified with Lausanne, although his acceptance there was marginal and his successor, Pareto, was in important ways his opposite. After retiring he expressed his ideas on nationalizing land with unmistakable conviction and élan in his Études d'Économie Sociale, a compilation of previous writings. He pictures himself there as a faithful successor to Quesnay and other Physiocrats who had sought in vain to save and reform l'ancien régime at Versailles by substituting l'impôt unique on land for the inherited tangle of taxes on business and labor that were choking French enterprise and weakening the state. He singles out for special censure J.B. Say, whom he calls a sell-out.

At Lausanne, Walras turned to pure theory and mathematics. Unsatisfied with the equilibrium of individual markets equating supply and demand through price flexibility, Walras asked how the whole system works, when everything depends on everything else. Our authors compare this with Zen; one might also mention Alexander von Humboldt's pioneering work on what he called Kosmos, a predecessor of modern ecology. Walras, at any rate, put his case mathematically, satisfying a compulsion of economists to have a model they can call a proof, and satisfy physicists on interdisciplinary committees that economics is really a "hard science". He asked if he could compose an equation for supply meeting demand in each individual market, then solve them all simultaneously to prove that the whole system creates the best of all possible worlds. Then it is just a matter of having as many equations as unknowns. This became known as "general equilibrium" in contrast with the previous "partial equilibrium" of one market at a time.

Essentially general equilibrium is merely formalizing what is inherent in Adam Smith, and intuitively so evident one hardly needs to formalize it, but perhaps that was tit for tat. Smith had merely popularized what the Frenchman, Quesnay, had earlier essayed to state more formally, so Walras was merely reclaiming what was originally French anyway – except that Quesnay, aka "The French Confucius", owed a good deal to the philosophy of Lao-tze. Ideas are indeed transnational and intertemporal.

Anglophones got to know Walras mainly through the translations of William Jaffe of Northwestern University, who made a career of translating Walras. Jaffe replicated for Walras the experience of Gossen, that is, he translated the mathematics and ignored the works on land reform. In 1975 Jaffe did publish in The Economic Journal a short piece, "Leon Walras: Economic Adviser Manqué", wherein he refers to

Walras' ideas on land reform, but only in a demeaning, mocking manner, and with no reference to Walras' major works like Études d'Économie Sociale. No one has translated the latter into English (it is likely that Routledge will publish Jan van Daal's translation in 2010, and there is an extract in Hillel Steiner and Peter Vallentyne (eds.), 2000, The Origins of Left Libertarianism). Generations of students have thus come and gone thinking of Walras as another incomprehensible apologist for the ruling class instead of the radical land reformer he was. The idea that we can have land reform and free markets at the same time has been erased from the minds of economic thinkers and policy makers – it no longer even can occur to them, so successful has this kind of brainwashing been.

Some unfortunate lacunae in Walras' system are time and information. Simultaneous equations are, well, simultaneous, while markets and their adjustments are not. Capital is formed and depreciates over time, so any model based on simultaneity is acapitalistic. DCF valuation of land calls for forecasting both rents and interest rates over infinite future time, which would entail not just perfect knowledge but Divine omniscience, a tall order even in "pure" theory. Thus Walras' general equilibrium, at least as passed down by others, deletes both capital and land values from the economy, contradicting Walras' other work on land values – but making his work all too acceptable as the plaything of later model-builders and taste-dictators of the clerisy beholden to the ruling class of rentiers.

Scornik and Foldvary emphasize that Walras in his Études d'Économie Sociale showed that land rents and values, rather than wages and interest, capture the major gains of social and technological progress. At the present (2010) conjuncture of the giant swings of the land cycle one might note that land values fall as well as rise, and their instability, and their use as loan collateral, are problems, too. Henry George opened his major work on Progress and Poverty by calling it "an inquiry into the cause of industrial depressions", but did not develop that thoroughly enough to be remembered as a cycle theorist. Many of those who quote George today – and there are still a good many – are libertarians like Arthur Laffer, Jr., who use George selectively as though he were, like them, an enemy of all taxes, indiscriminately. It is to be hoped that the present generation of analysts will see and fill the need to use George to find the cause of depressions – and a cure.

Scornik and Foldvary conclude from the ill-treatment of Gossen, Wieser, Walras, and George that the geocratic establishment will reject, and induce intellectuals to reject, any variation on the theme of land nationalization. Suppression of Walras' radical works demonstrates, for them, how "the power of landownership drives publication and education" – i.e. how the geocracy controls the clerisy. There will always be some of us, including I think Scornik and Foldvary, who won't take that fate supinely. Indeed, Adam Smith himself scolded the landowners of England for their "indolence". He was not referring to their slack usage of their superabundant inherited lands, but their failure to grasp the Physiocratic principle of tax incidence, that all taxes of whatever kind are passed through to landowners in lower rents. Along with the taxes themselves, their Excess Burdens are also passed through, so the way to maximize rents is to adopt a tax without excess burden, namely a tax on rents.

Thus, by Smith, the most rational landowner will favor taxes that fall directly on land and thus are free of excess burdens.

Vilfredo Pareto is the fourth economist whom Scornik and Foldvary treat. It is not crystal clear why they picked him for this study, unless for contrast. He was, as they tell us, a "total reactionary" who supported Mussolini, and whom Mussolini patronized: i.e., he was a Fascist. That a person of such views should dominate economic theory today speaks volumes about the persons who weave the screens that filter admission to leadership in the profession – and the ovine majority who take their cues from such leaders.

Pareto advanced a claim that distributions of wealth and income are equally skewed in all times and places and under whatever tax regimes or other institutions. The claim is conspicuously untrue – one need only contrast Wisconsin and Florida, for example, as this writer has in "Rising Inequality and Falling Property Tax Rates" (in Wunderlich, Gene (ed.), Ownership, Tenure, and Taxation of Agricultural Land. Boulder: Westview Press, 1992). Scornik and Foldvary cite the case of Taiwan in the last half of the 20th Century. Yet learned professors soberly present "Pareto's Law" to graduate students along with its inference that any effort to abate the concentration of wealth and income must fail. Classical economics dealt with the production AND DISTRIBUTION of wealth. Neo-classical economists have slowly eased Distribution out of the curriculum, replacing it with Growth. Pareto taught that only "growth", overall growth, can ever ease the lot of the poor. In politics, this became "A rising tide lifts all boats".

Pareto threw out all interpersonal comparisons, thus undercutting the traditional case for progressivity in taxation. The traditional case was based on the intuitive idea of diminishing marginal utility: the more you have, the less you need more. It was based on proverbial wisdom dating back ages, as in Virgil's deploring auri sacra fames, the accursed lust for gold; or as in the story of King Midas. It was based on Hebrew prophets like Isaiah and Amos cursing those who "lay field to field until there be no place". It was based on military traditions of equal rations for each soldier. It was based on dozens of observers like Bentham who anticipated what is now called Maslow's "Hierarchy of Needs". It was based on Tolstoy's popular short story, 'How much land does a man need?". It was based on everyone's personal experience with life. It was so obvious, so intuitive, it seemed to need no philosophical or mathematical "proof".

Pareto, like a clever lawyer, put the burden of proof on the other side, and the clerisy has followed. How can you prove, he asks, that taking an ounce of the miser's gold to save the lives of a hundred starving widows or trapped quake victims will raise the sum of human welfare? It seems never to have occurred to any leading economist to raise the obvious reply: how can you prove that the inherited distribution of land, based on bloody history and sinful chicane, is better than any alternative distribution? Without interpersonal comparisons one can't prove anything, so it's back to diminishing marginal utility. This involves feelings of empathy, common humanity, and brotherhood.

Scornik and Foldvary go on with Pareto at some length, justified more by his reputation and influence within the profession than by his merits. They are able by diligent searching to extract a few concessions from Pareto on the unique characteristics of land, but then find many reservations, leaving "an ocean of confusion and contradictions".

In summary, the authors show us how the filters of mediocrity and timidity have screened out the bold causes that three talented economists tried in vain to pass along to our generation. They also show how these same filters let pass the ideas of one Fascist economist to remold the discipline in his image and name. They show how this Pareto's thoughts on the special status of land left only "an ocean of confusions and contradictions". The last is a fair characterization of mainstream economics today, helping explain its shame and uselessness in forecasting the present depression, and piloting us to recovery.

Mason Gaffney
California, 2010

ii. Foreword

The major challenges facing governments in the 21st century – social, environmental as well as economic - cannot be resolved without first locating policies relating to land and taxation at the heart of public debate. But that creates an ideological crisis for policy-makers, because their expert advisors suffer from an amnesia that is self-induced. They have been schooled into forgetting that land and the resources of nature, and the tax rules that determine the distribution of the nation's income, play a central role in our lives.

Once upon a time, the customs and practices which lawyers now call the tenure of land served to support the welfare of members of the community. This was a natural, ethical arrangement which derived from the way humans evolved. To survive, they had to respect their natural habitats. But some of the earliest civilisations forgot this principle - the right of equal access to land – which was a decisive factor in their collapse.

Our society has also abandoned the practices that are necessary to deliver both efficiency and fairness in the use of land. How did this come about?

The authors of The Marginalists remind us that, 25 years ago, I wrote in The Power in the Land (1983) that a kind of conspiracy existed to deprive most people of their right to a share in the land of their communities.

To untangle the mess in both the theory and practise of economics, we now need to develop a clear understanding of the classical concept of land and of the rent which people agreed to pay for its use.

The tradition among English speaking economists stretched from David Ricardo's formulation of the theory of rent in his Principles of Political Economy and Taxation (1817), through John Stuart Mill to Alfred Marshall, in Britain. In America the most notable contribution was by Henry George, a journalist who taught himself economics and published the trail-blazing Progress and Poverty in 1879. On continental Europe, the integration of land into economic theorising featured the economists who are the subject of this study by Fernando Scornik Gerstein and Fred Foldvary. How this rich tradition was excised from the minds of the practitioners of economics in the 20th century was investigated by Professor Mason Gaffney.

The abject failure of governance was repeatedly exposed from the 1930s Great Depression to the Great Recession of 2008/09. These events were predictable – and, in the case of the recessions of 1992 and 2010, they were predicted in good time for governments to take action. The politicians failed to act because, put at its simplest, they could not get their minds around the idea that anti-social behaviour in the market for land could terminate economic growth. Millions of people have lost their jobs in the downturns. Homes were also lost after families were lured by bankers into taking out mortgages they could not afford. That created the conditions for the downturns. What should be done during the upturn?

Once again, governments agonise over symptoms – such as the size of bankers' bonuses – rather than the root cause of unsustainable economic policies. At the heart of a strategy for reconstructing holistic systems is the proposal to re-socialise land as part of the package of policies to reduce the tax burden on people who work for their living. For Europe, some of the marginalists discussed in this volume advocated the re-nationalisation of land, which would then be leased to users on payment of rent. This socialist approach would not find favour in the Anglo-Saxon world, but the same outcome could be achieved if property rights were left untouched.

All that is necessary is for the community to charge the full rental value of the public services that it provides. This would yield sufficient revenue to make it possible to reduce taxes on wages and salaries.

Whichever formula for reform was adopted could be left to the preferences of individual nations. But the democratic debate that is needed before the tax shift could occur is not likely to take place until the experts who advise governments have re-learnt the economics of the land market.

Land is a unique factor of production. And because land is fixed in supply in the places where people prefer to live and work, rent as a flow of income behaves differently from the wages of labour and the interest paid for the use of capital.

A close study of The Marginalists will deepen people's understanding of the effectiveness of the crucial decisions that are made at the margins of the economy. The leads to the vision of prosperity and social stability which is within our grasp.

Fred Harrison
London, 2010

The Marginalists

I. Introduction

There is no doubt that what is known as 'the marginalist revolution' occupies a prominent place in the development of economic thought. Nevertheless, its assessment and the treatment it deserves varies substantially, depending on the different approaches to economic thought and its main figures.

There is total rejection by traditional Marxism, accusing the Austrian school of ignoring real society and the class struggle which they allege is characteristic of it:

> 'by replacing the relationships of production by the relationships between men and things, the economists of the Austrian School present all categories of capitalism as natural and eternal, resulting from man's relationship to the surrounding nature.'[1]

To Marxists, the relationships of domination and unfair distribution of wealth are the very essence of a market economy.

At the other extreme, there is a total acceptance, not without controversies, of the marginalist's postulates by neoclas-

---

1 N. Kataraiev - M. Rindina : 'Historia de las Doctrinas Económicas' –Editorial Cartago, Buenos Aires 1965. Pags. 569-575; translation by Fernando Scornik Gerstein.

sical economists, although some alleged principles were not actually stated by the marginalists, or if they were, it was in very different contexts and with very different connotations from those attributed to them by modern followers.

One of the subjects that Marxists always ignore and that contemporary neoclassicists prefer not to mention is the very special status that land – all natural resources (inputs) - has held in the thought of some of the most distinguished members of what has been called, in a very general way, 'marginalism'.

As an example, the Austrian economist Ludwig von Mises was very critical of the mathematical economics so dear to some marginalists, who were accused by him of diverting analysis with a method which should only be an aid and could be unhelpful in interpreting a complex reality.

With respect to the factors of production, i.e. categories of inputs, Mises states that the

> 'modern theory of value and prices is not based on the classification of the factors of production as land, capital and labour. Its fundamental distinction is between goods of higher and of lower orders, between producers' goods and consumers' goods... The law controlling the determination of the prices of the factors of production is the same with all classes and specimens of these factors.'

He adds:

> 'Classical economics erred when it assigned to land a distinct place in its theoretical scheme. Land is, in the economic sense, a factor of production, and the laws determining the formation of the prices of land

are the same that determine the formation of the prices of other factors of production. All peculiarities of the economic teachings concerning land refer to some peculiarities of the data involved'. [2]

Mises deals but briefly with the theses of the physiocrats, even the great Turgot, and the major classical economists, Adam Smith, David Ricardo, and the two Mills. Without naming him, Mises dispatches Karl Marx, who devoted a substantial part of Volume III of Das Capital to a very precise study of the rent of land and considered the concept of private property of the planet the basis of capitalist exploitation. Mises also omits important aspects of original neoclassical thinking, from earlier writers such as Arsene Dupuit and Hermann-Heinrich Gossen to figures such as that of his fellow Austrian, Friedrich von Wieser, and the exceptional work of the French economist Leon Walras, the mathematical culmination of the marginalist revolution.

They all viewed land – all natural resources - as a distinct factor of production, different not only due to terminology, as von Mises seems to indicate, but based on a precise observation of reality, and in the case of Walras, by a solid economic-mathematical analysis. As the contemporary American economist Mason Gaffney has said, the classical economists knew very well what they were saying when maintaining that landed property is a monopoly. Marx also acknowledged it when he proposed in his Manifesto the nationalization of land as the first step in his program towards communism. And the neoclassicists that we shall study here

2 Ludwig von Mises: La Acción Humana. Unión Editorial S.A. Madrid 1986, pp. 925-929; cf. Human Action, Chicago: Contemporary Books, 3rd ed., 1963, pp. 636-7.

also recognised it, although some of them, like Pareto, without complete clarity.

In fact, they could not ignore what any normal person knows from their own experience, without any need of economic knowledge: that land, meaning all nature external to man, is indeed distinct. It has not been 'produced' by human action, but pre-exists mankind.

Unlike a building or tool, the price of land is not dependent on a 'cost of production' – it has none. The value of a plot land does not depend on what the owner happened to pay for it. From the viewpoint of society or the economy, land does not have an economic cost. That is because, since land is here by nature and not produced by human action, nothing had to be given up in order to provide land. Unlike labour, there is no "opportunity cost to land," as no resources or benefits such as leisure are given up or sacrificed to have land. An individual buyer has a cost of buying land, since he could have obtained something else, but for the economy, this is just a transfer of title and money, with no sacrifice of other resources.

The value of land is distinct from the value of the investments on the site; such improvements are capital goods, not part of the land itself. The market value of land depends exclusively on the expected future rents, whether explicit or implicit, that the owner can obtain. The price of land, generally speaking, is formed by its expected future rent capitalised at the current real interest rate.

Certainly it is true, as pointed out in the final decades of the XIX Century by Henry George – whom von Mises never even mentions – that land in strategic locations, for example in the centre of large cities, has an exceptional value:

> *'Land as land, or land generally - the natural element necessary to human life and production - has no more value than air as air. But land in special, that is, land of a particular kind or in a particular locality, may have a value such as that which may attach to a particular wine-glass or a particular statue; a value which unchecked by the possibility of production has no limit except the strength of the desire to possess it'.*

He adds:

> *'Where land is monopolized and the resort of population to unmonopolized land is shut out either by legal restriction or social conditions, then the desire to use particular land may be based upon the desire to use land generally, land the natural element; and its strength, measured in the only way in which we can measure the strength of a desire, the willingness to undergo toil and trouble for its gratification, may become when pushed to full expression, nothing less than the strength of the desire for life itself, for land is the indispensable prerequisite to life, and "all that a man has he will give for his life."*[3]

Hence, what we shall examine in this paper was not a mistake of the classical economists and, in this aspect, neither a mistake of Marx or of the neoclassicals. The deficiency is that of Mises and some of his followers as well as of contemporary economists of the neoclassical and various other schools of

---

3 Henry George: 'The Science of Political Economy'. Robert Schalkenbach Foundation, New York 1981. Pp. 255-256

thought. We live under a system, so-called "Western capitalism", in which, since spatial land is in the classical sense monopolized (as new land cannot be produced or imported), those 'peculiarities' that according to von Mises were due to specific data are not merely local variations but encompass a fundamental distinction for land.

It is indeed true that the supply and demand mechanism establishing the price of land in a market is the same as that establishing the price of capital goods, but in the application there is a critical difference: the amount of capital goods may be increased indefinitely. This is not the case for spatial land, its supply being fixed. The impossibility of importing or expanding land exacerbates speculation that increases the price of land beyond that warranted by current use, raising the cost of access to land. Therefore, in a progressive society, as Leon Walras pointed out, an increase in population increases the demand for land. The outcome is that the marginal utility of land increases: 'The intensity of the final desired satisfactions or "rareté" [marginal utility] of the consumed rents directly keep growing in a society step by step in parallel with the increase of population. Parks and gardens diminish their extension, houses are higher, the apartments, the corridors, the stairs grow narrower. In this way the value of rent grows in a progressive society: so it should be and so it is. In this case as in many others it is enough to substitute the consideration of the rareté which is an absolute element for the consideration of the value which is a relative element, to clear any doubt'.[4]

---

4 Leon Walras: 'Ètudes d'Économie Sociale'. Auguste et Leon Walras –'Oeuvres èconomiques complètes', Volume IV pages 323-324; translation by Fernando Scornik Gerstein.

Later we shall see the solution proposed by Walras to this problem, which he considered central in contemporary society.

Undoubtedly von Mises knew the works of Leon Walras, but maybe, like many others, including French economic historians who consider Walras as one of the greatest economists of all times, he did not recognize the importance to the part of his theory dealing with land, despite the importance accorded to land by Walras along with the classical economists.[5]

Before entering further into the thought of these economists, some concepts need to be clarified, starting with marginal utility, an essential category of marginalist theory. We begin with an example from Eugen Böhm-Bawerk (1851-1914), an Austrian economist, of course a marginalist, who gained fame for his theory of interest and also for his precise criticism of the method which Marx presented for the determination of prices that stem from production.[6]

---

5 Jean Boncoeur and Hervé Thouement in their 'Histoire des idées économiques'- Nathan-Paris-2000, Volume II page 8 state: 'Although Walras gave great importance to land in his works of applied economic and social justice, advocating the nationalization of land, it is essentially his contribution to pure economics –which he considered a natural science or even more a branch of mathematics – which granted him his fame for posterity. Because of his theory of value and marginal utility similar to those of Jevons and Menger, but worked out independently from them, and especially for his theory of general equilibrium, Walras is considered today one of the greatest economists of all times. Yet, Walras was long ignored, even in his own country" (translation by Fernando Scornik Gerstein and Fred E. Foldvary)

6 Marx perhaps would not have published in the same way, had he been alive, the 3rd volume of "The Capital", which was published by Engels. The algorithm of transformation presented by Marx for the construction of production prices contains a logical mistake that he recognized, but without giving any importance to it. As Jean Boncoeur and Hervé Thouement point out in 'Histoire des Idées Économiques' (Nathan, Paris, 2000, Volume I, pag.190/192), it is "probable that the author (Marx) was not entirely

Suppose, explains Böhm-Bawerk, that a farmer, distant from any road, has just harvested five bags of wheat, with which he has to survive until the next harvest. He needs one bag of wheat for subsistence. He uses the second bag to improve

satisfied with the analysis contained in his manuscript" (translation by Fernando Scornik Gerstein).

The development of the process of production that he presents in this way:

$P_i = (C_i + V_i).(1+R), i = (1, ..., n)$

is, according to the above mentioned authors, "logically inconsistent".

In this formula P is the prices of production, C_i and V_i respectively the 'constant capital' and the 'variable capital' (names that Marx gave to labour engage in production) used for the production of a certain good i, representing $.(1+R)$, the general (or medium) rate of profit.

Actually, the variable on the left of the equality is a price of a good, but the elements of the material cost and labour cost that appear in the right are expressed in values. If companies sell their products at the 'price' (cost) of production, they cannot buy the means of production for their alleged 'value'. The coherent expression of the system requires that both the output and the inputs of each activity are expressed in terms of alleged 'prices of production'.

It is interesting to follow Marx's reasoning in reaching this rejected formula. Consider an economy in which 'n' goods are produced. Assume that industry is competitive. To simplify, assume there is no fixed capital (thus, anticipated capital is consumed capital). If we designate C_i and V_i the constant and variable capital and PL the surplus value ("plusvalue") extracted from this production, the value of good "i" is

$C_i + V_i + PL_i , i = (1, ..., n)$

The total value of the advanced capital and the total value of the plusvalue extracted in the economy, would be respectively

$\Sigma C_i + \Sigma V_i$ plus ΣPL_i

from where the medium rate of profit resulting or the system of values would be

$R = \Sigma PL_i \ / \ \Sigma(C_i + V_i)$

which Marx uses to build the system of production prices . In fact, he writes the price of each good as the addition of its cost of production :

$C_i + V_i$

plus the medium profit, that is the profit calculated applying the advanced capital to the general profit rate:

$R. (C_i + V_i)$

This comes to

$P = (C_i + V_i).(1+R), i = (1, ..., n)$

The first one to point out Marx's error was the Austrian economist Eugen Böhm-Bawerk in his book Karl Marx and the Closing of his System, 1898. His conclusion was that the transformation of values in production prices proposed by Marx was a failure and as a consequence all the theory developed in Volume I of Capital is wrong. Perhaps that was too radical a conclusion.

his diet, the third to feed his poultry, and the fourth to distil liquor. With his most important needs covered, he uses the fifth bag to feed his parrot.

Böhm-Bawerk points out that various uses for the wheat do not have the same importance for the farmer. He places the greatest importance, hence degree of utility, to the preservation of his life. Using arbitrary numbers, Böhm-Bawerk establishes the utility of the first bag of wheat as 10 and the others successively 8, 6, 4 and 1.[7]

With such an example, marginalists express in a model what everybody knows using common sense: that when the most important needs are met, the subjective value of additional amounts diminishes. In the words of two Soviet economists:

> *'The degree of saturation of necessities depends on the quantity of goods available to the subject. If the quantity is unlimited and surpasses what is necessary to satisfy all the needs people have of them, then those goods will have no extra subjective value at all, even if the total amount is useful. Hence, for the economists of the Austrian School, the value of objects does not depend on their total utility, but on their available quantity and the marginal utility of the next item. The larger the quantity, the lower shall be the subjective value of the last unit. In the use of the five wheat bags, the value of the last unit equals 1. However, for the farmer, any of the five*

---

7 E. Böhm-Bawerk. Fundamento de la Teoría del Valor de los Bienes Económicos. 1929.

Leningrad: p. 20 (mentioned by N. Kataraiev, M. Rindina. op. cit., p. 573)

> *bags will have the same subjective value, because if*
> *he should lose any of them, he would not be able to*
> *satisfy the least necessity, that is, to feed the parrot.*"[8]

Actually, this is not a totally correct description of Böhm-Bawerk's idea. What really happens is that in the market, the total value of the objects does depend on the total utility, but the market price depends on the subjective value of the next unit after the last unit, rather than of the whole amount. The bags have differing subjective values, but what matters for the price is only the next unit, given all the previous units one has obtained.

The first theorist to analyse the concept of 'marginal utility' was not an Austrian, but a Frenchman: Arsene Jules Etienne Juvenal Dupuit (1804-1866), although the first to use the name was the Austrian Friedrich von Wieser (1851-1926). Others used the term 'utility on the limit', while Leon Walras (1834-1910) preferred the word 'Rareté', and Vilfredo Pareto (1848-1923) used the word 'Ophelimitè'.

The notion of 'marginal utility' is one of a family of 'great marginals': the margin of production, the marginal product of factors such as labour, marginal cost, marginal revenue, etc., as marginal analysis became part of the foundation of modern economic theory.

In spite of the fact that some marginalists are far from being totally clear, we do not think that the criticism of the American economist Henry George's[9] of Jevons, Marshall, Böhm-

---

8 N. Kataraiev. M. Rindina. Op. cit., p. 574 (translated with paraphrasing by F. Gerstein).
9 Henry George (1839-1897). One of America's most original economists and social philosophers. He proposed in his famous book "Progress and Poverty" the socialization of land rent by means of taxation, suppressing all other taxes and making of the rent of land the only source of revenue for the State.

Bawerk, von Wieser, Menger, and the Austrians in general, in the sense that they did not distinguish between value in exchange and value in use, is correct. They do distinguish one from the other, and they make the value in exchange dependent on the 'marginal utility', that is, on the value in use 'at the edge'.

They did indeed find the confluence between value in use and value in exchange, and with that they better explained puzzles that classical economists such as Adam Smith had raised, such as the famous example of water versus diamonds, water having a high degree of total utility but in most places a very low exchange value.

Certainly most marginalists have tended to confound land and capital, thus contributing to blurring the distinct character of land as an economic factor. As will be discussed in more detail later, the artillery of the American neoclassical school of thought was based on merging land and capital goods, and aimed against the classical theory of Henry George, who in emphasizing the significance of land, was seen in the final decades of the 19th century as the most dangerous challenge to the power of the ruling classes, Marxism being accorded very little importance in those days. Henry George's criticism regarding value is mainly addressed to this misleading intention, which was the one which in the end prevailed.

Marginalism, and the microeconomic analysis on which is based, was the outcome of a gradual evolution of thought developed during the 19th century simultaneously in different countries and by independent thinkers, some of whom were not even in the academic community. The predecessors were French (Cournot, Dupuit), German (Gossen), and earlier, Spanish scholars of the "School of Salamanca". Many of the concepts of the neoclassical school originated with the Austrian economists, which later became a distinct school of thought, as some of its important aspects have still not been absorbed by the mainstream neoclassical school.

Jevons was British, Walras was French, and Pareto was Italian. These, together with the Austrians Menger, von Wieser and Böhm-Bawerk, were significant names in the neoclassical revolution. There were also American neoclassicals: Clark, Seligman, Walker and others, as well as, following Jevons, Britons such as Wicksteed, Marshall and Pigou.

We shall now continue with the study of the four authors we have chosen, beginning with Herman-Heinrich Gossen.

II. Hermann-Heinrich Gossen (1810-1858)
The original thinker

The German economist Hermann-Henrich Gossen was the first to develop a comprehensive theory of consumption based on the marginal principle. He was a tax adviser for the Prussian Government, a position from which he was already retired when he wrote and published his fundamental book '*Entwickelung der Gesetze des menschlichen Verkehrs, und der daraus fliessenden Regeln für menschliches Handeln*' (The Development of the Laws of Exchange among men, and of the Consequent Rules of Human Action). The book was published in Brunswick in 1854 as a volume of 277 pages, organized in two parts, 'pure theory' and 'applied theory'. It remained unknown for years until in 1879, when it was rediscovered by W. Stanley Jevons. Gossen, sick with tuberculosis, died in 1858, extremely disappointed and certain that his ideas, which he considered (and which undoubtedly were) of high value, would never give prominence to his name.

As Robert Ekelund and Robert Hébert point out, his pure theory 'attracted attention due to its early formulation of the laws that have been named 'laws of Gossen'. The first law states the principle of diminishing marginal utility, to which he gave a graphic expression; the second describes the conditions for maximizing utility: to maximize utility, a given quantity of a good should be distributed in its different uses in such a way that marginal utilities are the same in every use'. [10]

In the second part of his book he puts forward a "geoclassical" theory. The term was coined by Fred Foldvary (1994) for classical theory, such as by Henry George, that recognized the significance of land. Gossen's treatment of land possibly explains the 'oblivion' the book was left in for years, and which is not usually mentioned by scholars who are always ready to jump over the thorny subject of land ownership. The ignoring and submerging of land is not only the 'great conspiracy' mentioned by Fred Harrison,[11] but part of the betrayal of economic thought as a social science, as pointed out by Mason Gaffney and Fred Harrison in '*The Corruption*

---

10 Robert B. Ekelund- Robert F. Hébert: 'Historia de la Teoría Económica y de su Método', McGraw Hill Interamericana en España S.A. Madrid 1992, p. 338/339 (translated by Fernando Scornik Gerstein).

11 'The mistake made by the founding fathers of the Industrial Revolution in the 1780's ... was to accept and institutionalise land monopoly. The British people, from the Clyde in Scotland to the Thames in the south-eastern corner of England, brought together human skills and material resources in an unique combination, and built a new economic edifice on a corrupt foundation... We do, here, identify a grand conspiracy, in the belief that the evidence is forthcoming to substantiate the charges. The specific allegations are that land monopolists since the Industrial Revolution have systematically prevented the public from undertaking those inventories that would lift the veil of secrecy that surrounds the land market, that this has been the greatest antisocial conspiracy in modern history...' Fred Harrison, 1983, The Power in the Land. London: Shepheard-Walwyn Ltd.: pp. 11 & 33.

of Economics', in the confrontation of the American neoclassicals with Henry George.[12]

Gossen states that

> *'it would be convenient that the ownership of land would belong entirely to the community, and that the community would grant the exploitation of each plot to whomever offered to pay the highest rent.'*

Commenting on his ideas, Leon Walras says:

> *'as pure a utilitarian as J. Stuart Mill, he backs this proposition with reasons of interest more than reasons of justice. He based this idea mainly on this principle that he tried to establish mathematically in his theory of economic equilibrium: that the highest rent corresponds to the most useful use. The State, holding all land in its hands, will rent plots to petitioners in certain conditions that he mentions and that according to him are justified... I shall mention only one, which is essential to consider here because it gives us the tool to perform the ideal. The rent to be paid by the tenant to the State shall increase year by year by a percentage as indicated by experience'.*

---

12 Mason Gaffney states: 'To most readers, probably George seems too minor a figure to have warranted such an extreme reaction. This impression is a measure of the neoclassicals success: it is what they sought to make of him. It took a generation, but by 1930 they had succeeded in reducing him in the public mind. In the process of succeeding, however they weakened the discipline, impoverished economic thought, muddled the minds of countless students, rationalized free-riding by land owners, took dignity from labour, rationalized chronic unemployment, hobbled us with today's counterproductive tax tangle, marginalised the obvious alternative system of public finance, shattered our sense of community, subverted a rising economic democracy for the benefit of rent takers, and led us into becoming an increasingly nasty and dangerous divided plutocracy'. Mason Gaffney, 1994, 'Neoclassical Economics as an Stratagem against Henry George' in The Corruption of Economics, Eds. M. Gaffney and F. Harrison. London: Shepherd Walwyn, in association with the Centre for Incentive Taxation: p. 30.

The method –comments Walras- would be the following: "If a is the rent in a given moment, z the annual rate of increase, an the rent after a certain number n of years, would be $an = a\ (1+z)^n$"

Based on an annual growth in value that he estimated for Prussia as 1%, Gossen considers it possible to pass all lands to the hands of the State. This plan, Leon Walras continues, 'so carefully drafted and thought out, reveals, in spite of the gaps that we indicate and that without any doubt could not be avoided in the first study of such a complex matter, not only an erudite with a deep knowledge of economic laws, but also an expert business manager'.

Gossen criticises the violent methods proposed by socialists and communists and denies the right for the State to expropriate land. The State should acquire land from the owners with respect also for the right to the growth value, as they had that in mind when they bought it. He maintains that the acquisition by the State is perfectly feasible, as it is in a much more advantageous position than individuals based on conditions that Walras summarises as follows:

1) The State may take loans with better conditions than individuals and, as a consequence, can pay a higher price for the purchase.

2) It has a much longer life and, as consequence, an amount to be cashed in the long run more value has for the State than for individuals.

3) For the same reason, the State may enter into long-lease contracts and as a consequence, get better returns'.[13]

13 Leon Walras: 'Etúdes d'économie sociale', Economica-Paris 1990. Page 229 (translated with paraphrasing by Fernando Scornik Gerstein and Fred E. Foldvary).

According to Gossen, the outcome of those three conditions is that 'the State may purchase land from individuals at a sufficiently low price to obtain from the increase of the economic rent the means to pay back the price of the purchase.'[14]

Gossen, who was undoubtedly a pioneer, suffered a bitter deception by the way in which his book was ignored. He had a high esteem, totally shared by Walras, for his theories (he compared himself to Copernicus), but perhaps he was ingenuous enough to ignore the powerful interests affected by his land-nationalisation proposition. We believe it was this proposal and not the 'laws of Gossen' that caused his book to be set aside.

When it was re-discovered, it was to praise its mathematics aspect, not his proposals for the purchase of land by the state (except, of course, for Walras, who shared his ideas in connection with land).

As Leon Walras said: 'it seems that a fatal flaw burdens this great problem' and that this would be the reason for such 'a very advanced mathematic theory of social wealth and such a remarkable theory concerning the attribution of the leases to the State' and 'one of the most beautiful books of political economy ever written', to be still completely ignored even in Germany'. [15] (For Walras, "social wealth" consists of things that can have prices or a value of exchange relationship among them.)

We can now see that it is not a fatal flaw that burdens

14 Leon Walras: Ibid: 258-260 (translated with paraphrasing by Fernando Scornik Gerstein and Fred E. Foldvary).

15 Leon Walras – Ibid: 231-232 (translated with paraphrasing by Fernando Scornik Gerstein and Fred E. Foldvary).

this 'great problem', but the powerful interests affected who defended themselves in the past, just as they defend themselves today whenever the subject of landed property is even touched.

Walras did not ignore this problem. In a noteworthy paragraph, he wrote:

'If in the second or third century of our era, a stoic philosopher had given the exact and precise formula of a social condition without slavery, with ways and methods to emancipate the slaves,[16] people with short vision and with good reasons to be satisfied with the existing order would find easy to demonstrate that his plan was in contradiction with the entire organisation of Roman society and maintain that in any case such formula would be never taken into practice, notwithstanding that this philosopher would have the truth and the future. So it happens with Gossen's theory on the repurchase of lands by the State with the redemption of the purchase price by means of the land leases. And so, to the glory of Copernicus that he claims and that is due to him for his conception of the mathematic equilibrium of the economic world, Gossen adds, according to my opinion, something of Newton for

---

16 The Stoics were the only school of philosophers of the Ancient world that critized slavery. Notorious were Lucius Annaeus Seneca (4 BCE – 65 AD), a Roman born in Cordoba, and Epictetus (50-138 AD), born in Hierápolis (Frigia), who taught in Epirus. Seneca was a teacher and minister of Nero, who, as a consequence of political intrigues, ordered him to commit suicide. According to history, Séneca opens his veins in absolute calm. Epictetus was himself a freed slave, and it is said that when he was under slavery, his master broke one of his legs. He dedicated himself to physics, logic and especially to ethics, but this doctrine is only known through the class notes of his disciple Arriano de Nicomedia. The stoics indicted slavery, and although in the first and second Century AD their doctrines were popular among roman nobility, the only practical effect in connection with slavery was a somewhat more benign treatment of slaves, such as the prohibition of killing a slave.

the solution of the social problem. Having said this I do not have one word to add to express my opinion on his merits' [17]

Like Gossen, Walras suffered from not having all his theory appreciated. Although aware of the difficulties his own theories had to face, was nevertheless greatly disappointed when the Nobel Peace Prize (the Economics one did not then exist) was not granted to him, after having been nominated.

We must now leave Gossen, due to the limitations of space, but not without hailing this lonely thinker, undoubtedly the first organic marginalist in the history of economic science, whose ideas about the differential character of land ownership were not only ignored by many neoclassicals, but distorted by others who took into consideration certain parts of his theories and put aside other ones, those which could present problems for their ruling-class patrons.

---

17 Leon Walras: Ibid: 326 (translated with paraphrasing by Fernando Scornik Gerstein and Fred E. Foldvary).

III. Friedrich von Wieser (1851-1926)
The realistic and progressive thinker

Born in Vienna from aristocratic parents, Friedrich von Wieser was Minister of Commerce of the Austro-Hungarian Empire in 1917. He studied economics at the Universities of Heidelberg , Jena and Leipzig.

The object of this essay is not to analyse exhaustively the ideas of any of the economists we have chosen, but to analyse how they treated land (in the widest sense) as a distinct economic factor.

In the case of von Wieser, an economist of extraordinary broad-mindedness and exceptional importance, this constraint regrettably prevents us from entering into some important aspects of his ideas, such as having originated the concept of opportunity cost as the real economic cost, a concept that mainstream economics has adopted as a core principle.

In spite of his aristocratic origin and his relations with the imperial government, he was an economist who paid more attention to the real economy and to the great differences in the purchasing power of different individuals.

Anticipating the ideas of the American economist Thorstein Veblen, Wieser points out that in a real economy, 'instead of the things that would be more useful, the things that are produced are those that are better paid. The larger the differences in wealth, the greater are such anomalies in production. Luxury is provided to the capricious and the gluttonous, while there is a dearth for those in misery and poverty. Hence it is the distribution of wealth that determines what is going to be produced and induces a consumption that squanders in culpable and unneeded indulgence what would have cured the wounds of poverty'.[18]

To demonstrate his theory, Von Wieser prepared a model of value such as it would exist in a communist country in which goods are valued simply according to the relation between the exiting quantity and the marginal utility. As Ekelund and Hébert, (whose study on Wieser we follow in this paper) point out: 'Although the Wieser model has a high degree of abstraction, based on this he reached a very important practical conclusion, one which with excessive slowness has also been reached by the practice of socialist countries. Wieser found that the prices of factors and goods play a fundamental role in determining the optimal allocation of scarce resources.'[19]

In my judgment, the most interesting of Von Wieser's

---

18 Natural Value, p. 58, cited in R. Ekelund and F. Hebert. Ibid: 351 (translated with paraphrasing by Fernando Scornik Gerstein and Fred E. Foldvary). Such statements are why contemporary Austrians, who emphasize efficiency and reject egalitarian concepts, refer only infrequently to von Wieser.

19 R. Ekelund and F. Hébert. Ibid: 351-352 (translated with paraphrasing by Fernando Scornik Gerstein and Fred E. Foldvary).

thoughts are the shadings he introduces to the Austrian theory of value that bring him near in a remarkable way to the ideas of Henry George and Leon Walras. Like George, he was a great defender of free trade as the way to press prices downwards.

When competition does not prevail, Wieser supported the intervention of the government to re-establish it. But what is more important here is his conception of the value relative to marginal utility for fixing the exchange value. He said:

> 'In an ideal and independent economy, the value of use depends on the utility and goods that are produced according to the order of their value. The value of exchange would in this case be the measure of personal acquisition. In a real economy the value of exchange depends not only on the utility but also on the purchasing power. The value of exchange in the real world does not necessarily follow the value in use or utility. In the real world, production is not fixed only by "simple necessity", but also by the superior means of a part of the population... In other words, prices in the real world do not normally reflect the valuations of the marginal utility that would exist if the marginal utility of the purchasing power were the same for all the individual claimants.' [20]

It is worth mentioning what he said about the rent of land:

> 'the rent of land is probably the formation of value most often attacked in today's economy. However, I

---

20 R. Ekelund and F. Hébert. Ibid 351 (translated with paraphrasing by Fernando Scornik Gerstein and Fred E. Foldvary).

> *think I shall demonstrate that even in a communist
> state, there must be rent of land. This type of state, in
> certain circumstances, must calculate the output of
> land and must calculate in certain portions of land
> a larger output than in other ones: the circumstances
> on which such calculation is dependent are essen-
> tially the same that fix the magnitude and existence
> of the rent. The only difference is that in the current
> circumstances, rent goes to the private owner of the
> land, which in a communist state would go to the
> whole community.*[21]

Actually, the latter and nothing more is what Karl Marx
proposed as point #1 in the program he proposes in the
Communist Manifesto, although many Marxists, including
those in power, thought that in a communist State, the rent
of land would disappear, since they read Marx as saying that
all value derives from labour.

What Wieser does not say in that context, although it is obvious, is that for the rent of land to go to the community, totally or partially, a communist State is not necessary. This is
what was proposed by James Mill, Henry George, Hermann-
Heinrich Gossen and, as we shall see, Leon Walras as well.
None of them was thinking of a communist State, all of them
writing for a policy that, in one way or another, paid the rent
to the community, some by taxation, others by nationalization to be followed by leasing to the highest bidders. Indeed,
Wieser too in his works on urban economics wrote of using
land rent for public revenue.

---

21 Natural Value, pp. 62-3. Cited in R. Ekelund and F. Hébert. Ibid: 352 (translated with
paraphrasing by Fernando Scornik Gerstein and Fred E. Foldvary).

As Ekelund and Hébert point out: 'to summarize, Wieser's analysis of value showed that the formation of value is a neutral phenomena. An understanding of natural value did not give any evidence in favour or against a socialist organization for society...the natural value was the basis of value in all societies, in spite of the fact that natural value could be concealed by other factors (such as controls, authorisations, great differences in purchasing power and monopolies). Wieser was one of the first economists to point out the generality of valuation based in utility and in a very clear way, the usefulness of the market system whatever the social organization.'[22]

These ideas of von Wieser motivated the criticism of those who, like Ludwig von Mises, thought impossible any accurate economic calculation in a communist system:[23] The historic reality of communist countries seems to have proven the reasoning of Mises to be correct.

Although Wieser, like the Austrians in general, underlined the role of marginal utility of final goods as the main factor determining the value, that is to say, as the source of value, he introduced in his analysis and with the variations that we have mentioned, a social theory that for many is a rationale for a 'welfare state'. He not only defended trade unions as a tool to avoid the exploitation of the workers, but also supported state intervention to protect the weaker sectors. 'Wieser was in favour of strong regulation and control by the state of companies partly because competition was not per-

22 R. Ekelund and F. Hébert. Ibid: 352

23 L. Von Mises 'La Acción Humana'. Unión Editorial Madrid 1986 - 319

fect and always because the revenues of big capital were not
entirely earned by the efforts of true and enlightened leadership.' Wieser offered as examples of unearned income the
urban rents raised by the increase in population and rents of
rural land in big farms, as well as the abuses in the shares and
speculation in the stock exchange.[24]

The appreciation of land, excluding improvements, is not
merely a possible case as is the abuses in companies by shares
or the speculation in the stock exchange, but a historic constant, excepting occasional recessions. The economic rent
and rise in land prices are always an unearned increment,
which owe nothing to the effort of the owner, but are a cre-
ation of a community.

Wieser reached important conclusions related to the influence of the exercise of power on welfare, and this is something near to Marxism. For von Wieser, the existence of monopolies of resources and products in the markets, and the
resulting stratification of utilities, prices and rents, should be
condemned. Nevertheless he concentrated on the compensating power of labour negotiation, anti-trust legislation and
free trade.

The authentic originality of Wieser is rooted in a combination of the Austrian theory of utility with a realistic and at the
same time evolutionary observation of society.

His thought, practical and with feet on the ground, should
undoubtedly be distinguished as an honest and progressive
approximation in the search for a solution to social problems, but far from a totally radical formulation.

---

24 R. Ekelund – F. Hebert. Ibid: 358 (translated with paraphrasing by Fernando Scornik
Gerstein and Fred E. Foldvary).

Let us now leave this particular thinker to enter into the mathematic and idealistic universe of Leon Walras.

IV. Leon Walras (1834-1910)
The mathematical and idealistic thinker

Leon Walras was born in Normandy, France in 1834. He always kept his French nationality, although he spent most of his life in Switzerland. Born the son of economist Auguste Walras, he not only inherited from his father the basis of his economic knowledge, but he also carried on his ideas during all his life, specially in reference to property in land.

He was not a brilliant student, nor an inspired youth. Walras obtained two bachelor's degrees, in letters and in science, but he failed in his intention to attend the Ecóle Polytechnique, one of the famous schools for French civil engineers. He finally entered a less prestigious school. He was also a frustrated writer of fiction, having in 1858 published what seems to have been a very bad novel. One thing is certain: these literary failures are evident in his writing, which is far from the high style of the likes of Adam Smith or Henry

George, although Walras did not lack strength or passion. Finally he decided to dedicate himself entirely to economics, but he couldn't find any academic position in France, basically due - as he himself points out indirectly when he mentions the sufferings of Gossen, - to his ideas about the nationalization of land.

Finally in 1870 he obtained, not without the opposition of three of the seven members of the nomination committee, a position as professor in the Faculty of Law in what would later be the University of Lausanne in Switzerland. From 1874 to 1877 he published the two parts of his Elements of Pure Political Economy, and in subsequent years he published The Mathematic Theory of Bimetalism, the Mathematical Theory of Social Wealth, and the Theory of Money.

In 1892 he abandoned teaching, publishing in 1896 his Studies of Social Economy and in 1898 Studies of Applied Political Economy, the two works being a compilation of previous writing, and which will be the basis for the analysis presented here. Walras died in 1910. He was by coincidence a contemporary of Henry George and he mentions George very briefly[25], but as far as we know, George didn't know him.

Walras was a solitary man of strong character, firmly attached to his ideas and dedicated to make them known, but unlike George, only in the academic world, through his copious correspondence with almost all the known economists

25 Walras mentioned George in his "Mathematical Theory on the Price of Land and its Repurchase by the State", along with Collins, Rodbertus-Jagetow, and Alfred R. Wallace, "as one of the many socialists I can mention who supported the right of the community over land". Leon Walras, Études d'economie sociàle (Studies of Social Economics), in Auguste and Leon Walras, Oeuvres Économiques complétes, Economica,. Paris 1990: book IX, p. 229.

of his time.

He had no faith in democracy, and could well have sub-
scribed to that phrase of the Argentinean writer Jorge Luis
Borges, 'Let me say that I disbelieve in democracy, that
strange abuse of statistics'. But neither did Walras have the
least respect for the French ruling classes, which in his view
had confiscated the Revolution for their benefit, resulting in
the economic ruin and decline of the nation. He believed that
the ruling class 'founded its fortune on the acquisition of national property at low prices, growing fat exploiting the char-
coal companies, the railways, and other monopolies, granted
always without regard for the public interest, these industries
being protected at the expense of consumers. Moreover, the
ruling class had not permitted the normal and regular teaching of social and economic sciences.'[26] As we can see, he was
an authentic iconoclast and in no way what Karl Marx called
an 'apologetic economist'. (In the sense used by Karl Marx).
Walras never renounced his ideas regarding land, which was
not the case of some others, such as Herbert Spencer, the
British 19th Century moral philosopher.[27]

While appreciating this strong and incorruptible scholar,
we must also add that sometimes the comprehension of his
thought is difficult. Rather than following it textually, what

---

26 Leon Walras, Etúdes d'economie sociàle. (Studies of Social Economics), op. cit., p. 420
(translated with paraphrasing by Fernando Scornik Gerstein and Fred E. Foldvary).

27 In his 1851 book "Social Statics", Spencer proposed the nationalization of land, so that
the rent would be used for public revenue, but in later Works he stated that due to difficulties in implementing equal rights to the benefits of land, there could instead be "joint
rights" to land, with individual ownership under the authority of the State. In his book "A
Perplexed Philosopher" Henry George criticized the deletion of the chapter, "The Right to
the Use of the Earth", from a 1882 edition of "Social Statics".

we shall attempt is to summarize his ideas, focussing on the theme of interest here, property in land. We will mention only tangentially his thought on what he calls 'pure or mathematical economics', his theory of general equilibrium, and the 'Law of Walras', as these are well known and respected by economists, and would take us far from our subject at hand.

To understand Walrasian thought in its complexity, we need to begin with his philosophical foundation, not always expressed clearly and precisely. We shall try to summarise it, following the method of the American sociologist cited by Walras, Franklin H. Giddings. In Giddings' view, the sciences are derived sequentially, on one level from the application of concrete and inductive sciences (chemistry, astronomy, geology, biology, psychology, sociology), and in turn from the abstract and deductive sciences (mathematics, physics, economic, ethics, and political science). For Walras there exists an abstract and deductive science which, following Giddings, he calls "cenonique genérale," a general theory that comprises pure ethics and pure economics. (It would be akin to what Ludwig von Mises would later called 'praxeology', an abstract, general, deductive science of human action).

Unfortunately it is not very clear what Walras intended to say. On the other hand, he is very precise when stating that 'economics, if it is not mechanics applied to equilibrium and the flow of social wealth, the way hydraulics is mechanics applied to the equilibrium and movement of liquids, is at least a science analogous to mechanics.' [28]

---

28 . Leon Walras, Etúdes d'economie politique apliquée (Studies of Applied Political Economy). Auguste and Leon Walras: op. cit: Book X p. 406 (translated with paraphrasing by Fernando Scornik Gerstein and Fred E. Foldvary).

Finally, and perhaps summarising too curtly, facing 'the
experimental illusion of human freedom as a fact of unique
importance',[29] Walras posits that there is a 'pure science'
which consists of the study of all the facts and propositions
for which the world is the theatre. We can call this, says Walras, 'pure natural science' or 'pure moral science,' according
to whether it is concerned with the works of nature or the
effects that flow from the exercise of human will.

Again unfortunately the alleged clarifications offered by
Walras are far from clear. He writes:

> *"Pure natural science results from the application
> of mathematics to physics, hence to chemistry and
> then to plant and animal physiology. Pure moral
> science results from the application of the "céno-
> nique" (abstract science that comprehends – as afore
> said – pure ethics and pure economics) to psychol-
> ogy, history, sociology, geography, and to statistical
> analyses".* [30]

This is reminiscent of how Ludwig von Mises would later
apply some basic premises of human action, such as the scarcity of resources and human action as purposeful optimiza-
tion, to pure, i.e. general and deductive, economic and social
theory.

As noted above, it is unclear exactly what Walras is seeking to say. What is fairly clear is that he states that there is
an overall "applied science" of humanity which he divides

---

29 . Leon Walras. Ibid. p. 408-411 (translated with paraphrasing by Fernando Scornik
Gerstein and Fred Foldvary).

30 Leon Walras. Ibid.,p. 410 (translated with paraphrasing by Fernando Scornik Gerstein
and Fred E. Foldvary).

into moral and natural categories, according to whether of the principles concern the ethical relations of persons with other persons, or else of persons with things. The moral science would be analysed from the perspective of justice, and the natural, from the point of view of utility. The first would be deductive; the second both deductive and experimental.

Applied economics would be the science that studies the relations between men not as moral persons but as economic actors who relate to their work or according to their relations with goods, a science that explains the laws regarding utility. Thus for Walras there is a branch of applied economic science independent of morality and exclusively based on utility, and another branch, the moral, based on justice. However, what should be emphasized is that the existence of separate branches does not imply that we can do without any one of these; the consequence of ignoring the moral branch has devastating effects for society, and just looking at the moral side without understanding the economic also leads to calamity. Just because the heart and brain are separate organs does not imply that we can understand the person only by examining one of these.

For Walras, the social scientist, pure or applied, should be differentiated from the statesman or the everyday man.

> 'The man of applied social science – we say - deduces from pure science an ideal organisation of society... The proper role of the statesman is to lead society towards the ideal indicated by the man of science. He should place himself in a relative point of view between the demands of science and the circumstances

*in which he finds himself. Any serious and lasting
social reform – we say - is a transformation between
the conditions of a point of departure and the conditions of the goals to which one desires to arrive".*[31]

The two indispensable disciplines would be 'a pure mathematical economics' under the inspiration of a 'general and
rational cénonique' by which to elucidate the just distribution of wealth.

Although the thought of Walras is subject to varying inter-
pretation, what is clear is that Walras applies mathematics,
i.e. logic applied in mathematical form, to the economy and
constructs his theory of general equilibrium and the law of
Walras on the foundation of the concept of marginal utility.
With respect to the social justice, Walras presents a solution
for the division of social wealth (that not due to individual
exertion) based on the nationalisation of land and the abolition of the prevailing tax system, a policy to which, as a man
of science, he attributes the character of an ideal we should
pursue, independently of whether we can achieve it.

Contrary to Marx, he considers that the socioeconomic
stages of history do not replace but rather become adjusted
to the previous ones. Walras analysed the social conditions
at the end of the 19th century as not only unjust but also
pointing to a bad prognosis for the future. Walras believed
that the ideal policies that he discovered should be like a
lighthouse guiding politicians towards needed reforms, although he himself taught that "never can we reach the ideal;
what is essential is to recognize it and strive towards it".

---

31 Leon Walras. Op. cit., p. 410 (translated with paraphrasing by Fernando Scornik
Gerstein and Fred E. Foldvary).

But, what is this ideal? To understand it, we need to see precisely something from his "pure applied economics", that is to say, from the mathematical part of his theory. We cannot, nor is it our intention to dig deeply into Walrasian theory, because this would take us into a very extended analysis, which in any case can be found in any history of economic thought.

It should suffice to point out that his fundamental contribution was the mathematical expression and explanation of the general equilibrium of the market. The basic economic concepts, the marginal approach, which he uses are the same as those used by Menger and Jevons, as well as Dupuit and others, for the development of the theories of utility and demand. But, as Ekelund and Hébert state: "Whereas these pioneers dealt with the functioning of utility and demand for only one good, Walras systematically presented a model for the maximization of the utility for an individual, given all the goods he consumes within the constraint of a budget. From these choices, could be deduced the individual supply and demand functions".[32]

Thus, the contribution for which Walras gained a place in the history of economic thought was precisely his mathematical formulation of a general system of equilibrium based on the criteria of utility, that is to say, on the entirety of taste or preferences related to the different possible collections of goods, constituting what is called a "utility function".

The concept of general equilibrium consists of all factors (land, labour, and capital goods) and all goods sold to house-

---

32 Ekelund and Hébert, Ibid., p. 456 (translated with paraphrasing by Fernando Scornik Gerstein and Fred E. Foldvary).

holds having prices and quantities such that at that moment, they are all in balance with one another, so that no prices or quantities are under any economic pressure to change. Walras expressed general equilibrium as a set of equations, each produced good being an independent variable as a function of all the other goods in the market. Aside from the mathematics, general equilibrium expresses the zen-like concept of all factors and goods being interrelated.

A fundamental concept in Walrasian theory is "marginal utility," which he called "rareté". As in contemporary neoclassical theory, it is the change in total utility to the individual from consuming an additional unit of a good. (In Austrian utility theory, marginal utility is the ordinal preference for one more unit of a good relative to more of some other good.) The "rareté" is a decreasing function of the quantity consumed. The marginal utility diminishes with a greater quantity.

Another important concept in the Walrasian universe is the ratio of the marginal utilities of two goods held. This ratio equals the 'marginal rate of substitution,' telling us how much more of one good has to be substituted for some reduction in the amount of the other good, to keep equal the level of total utility, thus keeping the person indifferent among the various alternative combinations. As one obtains more of one good, because of diminishing marginal utility, ever greater amounts of it need to be obtained to make up for the ever decreasing amounts given up of the second good. Given a budget constraint and the prices of goods, a person obtains that mix of goods that maximizes his total utility, and the marginal rate of substitution tells us what amounts of the goods the person will obtain to reach that maximum.

As Ekelund and Hébert state, 'modern economics is interested in maximizing behavior. Hence, it supposes that an individual will maximize his well-being, considering his preferences, circumstances, endowment of resources. Since resources are limited, the individual obviously cannot reach all the satisfaction he would like. As the economists say, he is under a budget constraint. The allocation of resources in a way that maximises utility is precisely what is identified by economists as rational behaviour'.[33]

One essential part in Walrasian general equilibrium consists of what has been called the Law of Walras. It is related to the concept of excess of demand and supply (more precisely, excess quantity demanded and supplied). Formulated simply, Walras' law states that with n markets (hence, n equations and n items), if n-1 markets are in equilibrium, then the nth market must also be in equilibrium. There cannot be a net excess quantity demanded or supplied for the whole economy.

As Ekelund and Hébert state, "Fundamentally the Law of Walras is a way of expressing basic interrelations in the economic behaviour of the individuals. It is a useful shorthand, which expresses the conclusion that considering the tastes of individuals and the constraint of the rent, the excesses of supply and demand for all goods must be equal to zero. In other words, the supply and demand for goods in real terms is not independent... Walrasian theory describes the neces-

---

33 Ekelund and Hébert, Ibid., p. 459 (translated with paraphrasing by Fernando Scornik Gerstein and Fred E. Foldvary).

sary interconnections among the factors markets and goods markets in an idealised competitive economy. The Law of Walras in consumption and in production... is a shortened expression to describe these interesting and fundamental interconnections"[34]

Ekelund and Hébert add: "the model of the system is precise, but Walras did not and could not undertake the comprehensive statistical investigation necessary to give empirical solutions to each of the equations of the system. As a matter of fact, formidable problems are posed when the time comes to specify the relevant equations in concrete terms and to put together the information in such a big scale. It should not be interpreted that recognising such problems diminishes the importance of the contribution of Walras". Although he was according to the opinion of these authors, a rather mediocre mathematician, Walras nevertheless demonstrated the power of mathematics to solve complex theoretical problems.[35]

With this brief summary we should now leave the mathematic environment of Walras to enter into his "ideal" world, to the policies he proposed for society. We venture into what he perhaps would call the fruits of his moral applied science, deduced from the propositions of what he calls "pure rational science."

There is nevertheless a point of confluence, which explains our brief incursion into his mathematical universe. The intersection from which both his theories diverge, that applied

---

34 Ekelund and Hebert, Ibid., p. 463-6 (translated with paraphrasing by Fernando Scornik Gerstein and Fred E. Foldvary).

35 Ekelund and Hebert, Ibid., p. 468 (translated with paraphrasing by Fernando Scornik Gerstein and Fred E. Foldvary).

based on utility and the applied based on justice, is precisely the concept of "rareté", of marginal utility.

As noted above, by "social wealth" Walras means things that can have prices or a value of exchange relationship among them. Social wealth is composed of "capitals" (things that can be used more than once or continuously) and perishable goods (consumer goods, or things that serve the user once, thus being consumed). Capitals are what are in English called factors, and comprise land, personal faculties (labour), and artificial (man-made) capital, the latter, says Walras, properly called capitals (or as the Austrian-school more clearly designates it, capital goods). The services of the capitals that have a direct utility plus the objects of consumption fall under the name 'consumable services', while those that only have an indirect utility, plus raw materials, fall under the name 'productive services.'[36]

Walras differentiates between a market of services and a market of goods, and 'on each market we may observe a rise in price in the case of excess of quantity demanded over the quantity supplied, and a decrease in price for the case of an excess of the quantity supplied over the quantity demanded. The state of equilibrium to which competitive markets tend but never reach would be that in which the quantities supplied and demanded of each service or good are equal, and in which the [marginal] cost of production and the selling price of each product are equal. That is the mechanism of free-market competition.' For Walras, pure economic theory

---

36 Leon Walras, "Etudes d'économie politique appliqué". Auguste and Leon Walras, Oeuvres economiques completes. Economica – Paris 1999 p. 416 (translated with paraphrasing by Fernando Scornik Gerstein and Fred E. Foldvary).

is a psychological-mathematical science:

> '*Only mathematics is able to demonstrate that we
> reach equilibrium prices corresponding to the equal-
> ity of the quantities supplied and demanded, prices
> rising when the quantity demanded exceeds the
> quantity supplied and decreasing when the quan-
> tity supplied exceeds the quantity demanded, and
> which arrive at the equality of the [marginal] cost
> of production and the sales price by increasing the
> quantity of products when the price of sale exceeds
> the cost and reducing the quantity of those products
> when the cost exceeds the price of sale*'.[37]

According to Walras, only mathematics can demonstrate
precisely that:

> '*the condition of utility maximization for the con-
> sumers is that the intensity of the final satisfied
> wishes (marginal utilities), after the exchange, are
> proportional to the prices,*' *from which it follows that*
> '*in the state of equilibrium, prices are proportional
> to the intensity of the last satisfied needs, or the mar-
> ginal utilities, for all consumers*', *and that* '*the price
> of a good increases if its marginal utility increases or
> if the quantity diminishes, and the price diminishes
> if the marginal utility diminishes or the quantity
> increases*".[38]

---

37 Leon Walras, ibid, p. 417 (translated with paraphrasing by Fernando Scornik Gerstein and Fred E. Foldvary).

38 Leon Walras, Ibid., pp. 417-18 (translated with paraphrasing by Fernando Scornik Gerstein and Fred E. Foldvary).

Briefly expressed, value is an increasing function of utility and a decreasing function of quantity. There may well be, as Ludwig von Mises pointed out, in Walras an over valuation of the role of mathematics in economics. Logic, not necessarily mathematical, is sufficient to make evident many of his propositions. We leave this to the judgement of the reader.

What is of interest here is an essential point in Walrasian thought: that in a progressive society wages do not necessarily increase and land rent necessarily increases. For Walras, even though rent 'is established in the market of productive services by reason of the offer by the land owners and by the demand either of the entrepreneurs who wish to use it to create products or the demand of consumers who desire to use it directly', necessarily 'the intensity of the final needs satisfied [by a plot of land] or the marginal utilities of the consumed rents keep growing in a society step by step with the increase of population', and he adds: 'the fact of the appreciation of the land rent in a progressive society is a fact well proved by experience and well explained by reasoning, from which one concludes that to leave lands to individuals, instead of reserving them for the state, implies allowing a parasitical class taking advantage of the enrichment that should instead satisfy the always growing demand for public services".[39]

This is the key point of Walrasian social and moral theory. If the value of land comes from nature and social effects, from the growth of society, why should we not leave the benefit for the whole society? Walras believed that it is very difficult to cure wrongs already created, but that we can improve

---

39 Leon Walras, "Etudes d'economie sociale" Page. 324 (translated with paraphrasing by Fernando Scornik Gerstein and Fred E. Foldvary).

the future. Hence, he proposes his mathematical theory for the repurchase of land by the state, which would then lease it out to the highest bidder. Following Gossen's prescription, Walras proposes to use the increase in the land rents it would receive (which corresponds to the appreciation of land value) to finance the purchase until fully paid for, and then the state would use the rent as a source of income.

In this way, "we would have not only saved the future but repaired the past". Although he sometimes uses the word 'expropriation', it is quite clear that his proposal is the purchase of the land by the state. He uses that word because the owners had in mind the appreciation when they bought their lands, and they expect that the appreciation should belong to them.

In reality, if not appearance, a person who purchases land purchases its future rents (implicit or explicit) and appreciation. The gains from population increase, technological progress, and public works go to a great degree to those holding title to land, while public revenue takes income that also bears having to pay the landlord for living space. Like Walras, we know that this is not the individual fault of landowners, but rather that it is the tax and land tenure system which is perverse and extremely difficult to modify. That the solution proposed by Walras has had the same scarce fortune as those proposed by Gossen or Henry George makes it evident that although they are quite different solutions to a similar problem, the rejection from the establishment is the same for any of the variations.

Let us now look at some of the questions raised by Walras. "Why we should allow that on one side landowners get ever richer, while on the other side, the "proletarians" (low-skill workers) get [relatively] poorer by the sole fact that society develops? There is no right against right, and there is no time limitation status in favour of an inequity which is always persistent...'

'The collective property of land, and the lack of taxes, which would be its consequence, are not only two acts of justice, they are acts of essential interest for a nation that wishes to live. Justice is not a luxury, as we would say of a painting that one is deprived of hanging in one's living room, if we have failed to purchase it; it is to society what health is to a human being, a thing the lack of which condemns society to obscurity and misery...

'Hence, if we have lost it, and wish to recover it, a regime, a treatment, an operation would be needed; it is necessary to undergo it. We must ask only one question: to know whether the sick person has the strength to support the treatment.'[40]

With respect to what we have commented about the rejection of these ideas by the establishment and in speaking about "official economics" and of particular economists of the "system" (whom Marx called "apologists"), Walras says to economists:

> 'If you dare to put yourselves apart from the accepted ideas, all the academies, all the societies, all the journals, all the newspapers will close their doors before you. On the contrary, if you give evidence of submission in the contests that are open before you

---

40 Leon Walras "Etudes d'economie sociale" Ibid., pp. 416-7 (translated with paraphrasing by Fernando Scornik Gerstein and Fred E. Foldvary).

*in this age in which the desire for fame and the need
of success are so acute, your fortune will be completely secured.*[41]

We have pointed out before his little faith in democracy:
"I truly do not believe that the democratic state we enjoy is
at the high stage of undertaking such a reform, but the value
of a social and economic theory does not necessarily depend
on the possibilities they may have to be immediately put into
effect.[42]

As we have aforesaid, he proposed an "ideal", and later it
would be the task of practical politicians to try to put it into
practice.

However, Walras could be contradictory. On one hand, he
affirms the injustice of the private appropriation of land rent,
but on the other hand, he affirms in his theory of property –
without establishing distinctions - 'that the owner of a thing
is owner of the services of that thing,' and since 'who may
do the most can also do the least,' he who has the immediate
right to a thing, has also the right to consume it in the long
run, that is to say, to consume its services.[43]

Walras does not say that this is only applicable to what he
calls the proper capital (the movables), but also includes land.
This explains why he proposes the repurchase of land and

---

41 Leon Walras "Etudes d'economie sociale" p. 424 (translated with paraphrasing by Fernando Scornik Gerstein and Fred E. Foldvary).

42 Leon Walras. Ibid., p. 326 (translated with paraphrasing by Fernando Scornik Gerstein
and Fred E. Foldvary).

43 Leon Walras, Ibid., p. 177-8 (translated with paraphrasing by Fernando Scornik Gerstein and Fred E. Foldvary).

not really its expropriation. He is very clear in this respect:

> *"The owner of capital, whether personal, movable, or immovable, is the owner of the rent, the work, or the benefit of this capital, and owner of the products he receives as lease, salary or interest in exchange for the service of this capital".*

And he adds: '... as a consequence it is sufficient for the theory of ownership to analyse just the distribution of returns on lands and personal faculties: all the social wealth will be ultimately distributed to these categories ...

> *'There are thus two types of social wealth to distribute: land and personal faculties, and there are two categories of society to which social wealth may be divided, the state and the individual. According to the principle of inequality of human traits, personal faculties should be attributed to the individual, and according to the principle of equality of conditions, lands should be attributed to the state. To say more than this is useless."*

Walras says that both conservative and socialistic economists have disregarded the central topic (whether because of lack of interest or lack of knowledge), which is the appreciation of land rent and land value resulting from the increase of the marginal utility of land in a progressive society... This is the theory of distribution of wealth based on justice.[44]

Walras states also that in the existing system the farmer and the landowner are usually two different persons, and that as a

---

44 Leon Walras, "Etudes d'economie politique apliquée", Ibid., pp. 421-3 (translated with paraphrasing by Fernando Scornik Gerstein and Fred E. Foldvary).

consequence a transformation of territorial individual property in collective property separating the roles of the farmer
and the landowner – that would be the state - would not only
be harmless but would be very favourable for production:

> *"to the contrary to what is said everyday, that in-
> dividual property has made nations come out of
> barbaric stages and that collective property of land
> would make them return to it, the truth is that na-
> tionalisation of the ground is always desirable from
> the point of view of transformation of agriculture.
> On the other hand, it is in the social interest to have
> collective property in land, while the social interest
> demands as well the plain and complete rights to in-
> dividual property, which implies the suppression of
> taxes [on labour and produced goods].*[45]

For Walras, this theory of property encompasses a theory
of taxation. The state as owner of the land should live on the
income of the land, using part of it for its current expenses
for public services, and using the rest in the formation of
capital goods in the public interest. In contrast, the theory of
taxation based purely on individualism has no way out:

> *'After having let all social wealth fall into private
> property, efforts to obtain the income of the state
> become futile. Just as the individual has no right
> to the rent of land, the state has no right to an indi-
> vidual's labour, wage, or products. It has no right to
> the capital, earnings or interest coming from labour.
> It has no right to any property other than the rent of*

45 Leon Walras, Ibid., p. 422 (translated with paraphrasing by Fernando Scornik Gerstein
and Fred E. Foldvary).

> land. I have maintained this thesis since the beginning of my career.'

Walras notes that although there is not a pre-established equality between the territorial rent and the financial needs of the state, there is a harmony in the fact that "the total amount of territorial rent increases or decreases with the population and wealth of the nation, and as a consequence with the financial needs of the state".

Some authors such as James Mill have thought that the income from land would exceed the needs of the government, while others, such as Charles Gide think that public expenditures need to be much higher than the income we can expect from ground leases. The position of Walras is that 'the income of the state is variable, and an adaptation [of spending to revenue] is possible.'

Comparing individuals with states, Walras writes that 'nature has given the land to all, and our personal abilities to each one. In accord with moral principles that can be deduced rationally from moral premises, I conclude that we should use ground rent in common and our wages individually. If we shift the land question from what is right to what is expedient within the status quo, we shall continue to let idle elites and indigents live at the expense of those who are industrious and efficient. We shall let the former indulge themselves at the expense of the state and the state at the expense of the latter.[46]

Passing to practice, he says that the first step, however in-

---

46 León Walras Ibid., p. 424 (translated with paraphrasing by Fernando Scornik Gerstein and Fred E. Foldvary).

complete, would be to establish and administer land-value taxation by the state as a co-owner of the land. This way the state would be assured its portion of the rent and its future increase.

In the system that he explains in his 'Mathematical Theory of the Price of Land and its Repurchase by the State,' Walras proposes that the state, without altering the basic elements of the land tax, "become in effect a co-owner. Thus, the state would already be a part-owner and would then purchase from landowners their part, compensating them with bonds. The state, finally, would lease lands that would belong to it, to renters whether they be households, farmers, or industrial and merchant tenants. The amount of interest paid on the bonds could exceed in the beginning the amount of the ground rent that it would receive from the leaseholds, but as the leases generally increase with each renewal, and the payments to individual owners diminish by the redemption of titles, the deficit would turn into a surplus. When this process reaches its finally stage, the state, owner of all the land, will thrive on leasing it, and taxes would be abolished. The modern world would have cured its social wound, a thing that the ancient world could not accomplish.'[47]

Walras says that by recovering lands for the state, we would confront and solve a primary social problem, the distribution of wealth among men in society, and, corresponding to this, preventing landowners from benefiting disproportionately from the increasing productivity of the economy.

---

47 León Walras Ibid., pp. 424-426 (translated with paraphrasing by Fernando Scornik Gerstein and Fred E. Foldvary).

The other social issue, in his view. would be to prevent particular industrialists from making extraordinary gains in violation of the canons of free-market competition, thus to hold down the pricing power of firms. The state, he says, should intervene to enhance competition (i.e. reduce pricing power), and when it cannot do so, it should undertake the activities directly itself or regulate the firms in the most convenient way. 'The inclination of landowners, workers and capitalists is to create a monopoly in the input services, and that of entrepreneurs is to form monopoly cartels for products. If the monopoly is contrary to the public interest, the state should impede these in every case that is not based on natural rights'.[48]

This anti-monopoly viewpoint is somewhat curious, since Walras indicates elsewhere that workers and owners of enterprises have a natural right to their freedom of enterprise and to their gains; perhaps what is meant, or should mean, is that the state should not protect such cartels from competition. Walras also perhaps under appreciated the dynamics of a free market, where the economic profits of cartels spurs entry into an industry and reduces the pricing and collusion power of the firms.

Walras differs sharply from Henry George on compensation to landowners, Walras believing that the title holders should be paid the market price, George being opposed to compensation. There is otherwise remarkable agreement on economic and moral theory and on policy. As noted above, George was unfamiliar with the ideas of Leon Walras or the similar ideas of his father, August Walras. Their writ-

---

48 León Walras . Ibid. pages 424/426

ings were not widely propagated in translation until after the death of George. If George and Walras had known one another, if they had corresponded and read each other's work, quite likely George would have much better appreciated the theoretical importance of marginal utility.

What is interesting in Walras is that his policy is not centred only on the theme of land to solve the social question. In addition, like George, Walras makes economic freedom - free trade, free markets, and competition - a foundation for his system. Like George, Walras paid homage to the French Physiocrats of the 1700's, who espoused free trade and the impôt unique, the single tax on land rent. For Walras, the free market is the general and superior basis for the production of wealth.

Walras declared, 'It will always be the honour of the first economists (the Physiocrats) to have recognised (and it will be our merit, that of the mathematical economists, to have demonstrated) that the free market is, within certain limits, a self-propelled and self-regulated means for the production of wealth, if we deem people capable of knowing and pursuing their interests, that is to say, that they are rational and free-willed persons. Given this condition, which is sound and legitimate, we shall demonstrate, as we have already seen, that in a free and competitive economy, prices and quantities spontaneously tend towards an equilibrium which maximizes utility and reflective of the scarcity of and value ascribe to resources.

'If the total amount of a good diminishes, its marginal utility increases, the price rises, and thus also the profit, so there is a benefit for the entrepreneur to produce more and increase the quantity. If the amount increases, the marginal utility diminishes, and the price comes down. There is a loss for the entrepreneur, who will produce less and reduce the quantity. All these processes flow from maximizing utility'... No applied science will know how to offer a general and superior rule with better proof than this one of the free market. Nevertheless, it bears repeating that to institute and maintain a competitive free market is a legislative task, one of complicated legislation, a task that necessarily pertains to the state.'[49]

For Walras, one condition of competitive private enterprise is that the individuals are free to increase their utility. The other condition is that the number of firms in an industry can freely increase. The first is not possible in collective services, and the second is not possible for natural monopolies. Such industries, he concludes, should be run by the State or under its supervision.

In connection with protectionism, Walras is crystal clear: 'regarding commerce, the great question put forward whether there shall be free international trade or else protection. Applied economics, based on pure theory, shows that free exchange, the essence of industrial and commercial activity, has only advantages and no harm, but only if the socialization of land and the suppression of taxes is also resolved.'[50]

As we can see, not only is Walras a supporter of free trade but also, just like Henry George, he relates its effectiveness to the socialization of land rent and the consequent abolition of taxes.

---

49 Leon Walras. Ibid., pp. 426-425 (translated with paraphrasing by Fernando Scornik Gerstein and Fred E. Foldvary).

50 León Walras - Ibid. Page. 426/429 (translated by Fernando Scornik Gerstein)

We hope in this brief and by no means complete study to have given a general vision of the ideas of this important thinker, whose analysis and policy regarding land are little mentioned, and mostly ignored, by historians of economic thought. That such important thoughts by such a prominent economist as Walras could be sequestered in such a way only demonstrates how much the monopolistic power of land ownership drives publication and education in our 'free' societies.

V. Vilfredo Pareto (1848-1923)
The reactionary theorist, efficiency expert, and pessimistic thinker

Italian economist and sociologist, it can be said that in reference to general equilibrium and the application of mathematics to economics, Vilfredo Pareto was a disciple and follower of Walras, who in fact nominated Pareto to succeed him in the chair of political economy at the University of Lausanne in 1893. He does not follow, however, Walras' ideas on land nationalization, being more inclined towards solutions based on taxation, although proposed in a rather diffuse and tangential way.

Pareto was, like Walras, at first an engineer, graduating from the Polytechnic University of Turin. His '*Manual of Political Economy*', published in 1906, contains his major contributions to economic science, including his theory of ordinal utility, his analysis of tastes and obstacles in the determination of value, his theory about the maximization of 'ophelimite' (a term he takes from Greek and with which he refers to 'marginal utility'), and a statistical theory about distribution of income, known as the "Pareto income curves" or 'Law of Pareto'.

Pareto's theory about the 'circulation of elites' is also notable, according to which every society is governed by an 'elite' that must renew itself perpetually, taking the best from the common people and expelling the 'degenerate' elements. A declared enemy of universal voting, he blames it, among other consequences, for 'a general increase in the morbid piety known as 'humanitarianism' and a notable increase in the indulgency and approval towards the bad customs of women'. [51]

As we can see, he was a total reactionary, only tempered by his honesty with respect to economic efficiency, as we shall see. Towards the end of his life Pareto supported Mussolini, who offered him a position in the Senate, which Pareto did not accept.

Regarding his famous 'income curves', Pareto said:

> *'Experience reveals to us a singular fact: that the curve of distribution of income has little variation, either in space or in time, for civilized societies for which we have statistical information'.* [52]

According to Pareto there is something in human nature, <u>which he did no</u>t identify, that causes an unequal distribution

---

51 Jean Boncoeur- Hervé Thouement: 'Histoire des Idées Economiques'. Nathan- Paris 2000, p. 53 (translated with paraphrasing by Fernando Scornik Gerstein and Fred E. Foldvary).

52 Vilfredo Pareto: 'Cours d'Economie Politique', Librairie Droz, Geneve- 1964- p. 408 (all quotations from Pareto have been translated with paraphrasing by Fernando Scornik Gerstein and Fred E. Foldvary).

of wealth. Whichever may be the system adopted, the curve will tend to return to its original position. Hence, the only hope for social improvement would come from economic growth. 'To increase the lowest level of income or to diminish the inequality of incomes, it is necessary that wealth grow faster than population. Here we may see that the problem of improving the conditions of the poorer classes is mainly a problem of the production of wealth.'[53]

This is really the theoretical basis of the modern theory of growth which, without touching the distribution of income, leaving all the inequalities as they are, centres around the efforts to fight against poverty using economic growth. It is the "official" ideology of development economics and policy as we begin the 21st century.   Differing from the English tradition (Marshall, Pigou) with its framework of partial equilibrium, Pareto built his theory of economic growth on Walrasian general equilibrium. Pareto pointed out some contradictions in Walrasian theory, especially concerning the determination of prices or exchange value.

For Pareto, the price 'is determined at the same time as the equilibrium and arises from the opposition between tastes and obstacles. He who does not look at more than one side, and considers only tastes, will believe that only tastes determine the price and shall find the cause for value in marginal utility. He who looks at the other side and considers only the obstacles will believe them to determine exclusively the price and shall find the cause of value in the cost of production, and if in among the obstacles he considers only labour, he

---

53 Vilfredo Pareto - Ibid. Page 408.

will find only in labour the cause of value.'[54]

> *'Such an oversight of the variables of production and their connection with the rest of economic phenomenon conveys serious errors. So it is that it is at times reasoned as if a cost of production could exist independent of the cost of products and other conditions of economy. Once that proposition is admitted, either explicitly or implicitly, one is tempted to deduce that the cost of production determines the sales price... We cannot abstract from the other circumstances of economic equilibrium and separately determine the cost of production. The cost of production is not the cause that determines the price of a good, just as it is not the selling price that determines the cost of production. These figures are simply related by certain conditions which if we add all other conditions of economic equilibrium will determine the unknown quantities of the problem.'*

Notwithstanding he also tells us that 'we should never forget that the conditions we have established for economic equilibrium define an ideal phenomenon that could be considered a first approximation to the concrete phenomenon.'[55]

It is interesting to compare Pareto's analysis with that made by Henry George in The Science of Political Economy (chapters XII, XIII and XIV):

---

54 V. Pareto: 'Manual d'Economie Politique', - Geneve – Droz. 1966- cap. 3.

55 Vilfredo Pareto: 'Cours d'Economie Politique'- Librairie Droz-Geneve 1964, page. 74, 694 and 645 of the Volume II contained in the same book. Also page 15 paragraph 596.

'It is not the toil and trouble which a thing has cost that gives it value. It may have cost much and yet be worth nothing. It may have cost nothing and yet be worth much. It is the toil and trouble that others are NOW willing, directly or indirectly, to relieve the owner of, in exchange for the thing, by giving him the advantage of the results of exertion, while dispensing him of the toil and trouble that are the necessary accompaniments of exertion' ... 'That which may be had without the toil and trouble of exertion has no value'... and he adds: '... Now, while the resistance to movement is inertia... so the resistance to the gratification of desire is the toil and trouble of exertion. It is this that is expressed and measured in values'... 'The value of a thing in any given time and place is the largest amount of exertion that anyone will render in exchange for it. But as men always seek to gratify their desires with the least exertion, this is the lowest amount for which a similar thing can otherwise be obtained... 'It is never the amount of labour that has been exerted in bringing a thing into being that determines its value, but always the amount of labour that will be rendered in exchange for it. Nevertheless, we properly speak of the value of certain things as being determined by the cost of production. But the cost of production that we thus refer to is not the expenditure of labour that has taken place in producing the identical thing, but the expenditure of labour that would now be required to produce a similar thing – not what the thing itself has cost, but what such a thing would now cost... 'Thus the point of equation between desire and satisfaction, or as we usually say, between demand and supply, tends in the case of things that can be produced by labour to the cost of production - that is to say, not what the production of the thing has cost, but the present cost of a similar thing. Desire remaining, whatever increases the amount of labour that must be expended to obtain similar things by making them will thus tend to increase the value of existing things; and whatever tends to decrease the cost of obtaining similar things by making them will tend to decrease the value of existing things... 'Cheapness or low value is the result of abundance; dearness or high value the result of scarcity. The one means that the satisfaction of desire may be obtained with little effort, the other that they can be obtained only with much effort. Thus there may be general increase or decrease of value as clearly and truly as there may be general scarcity or general abundance...

'Whatever increases the obstacles, natural or artificial, to the gratification of desire on the part of the ultimate users or consumers of things, thus compelling them to expend more exertion or undergo more toil and trouble to obtain those things, increases their value, whatever lessens the exertion that must be expended or the toil and trouble that must be undergone, decreases value.'[56]

Returning now to Pareto's analysis, we may see that George by focussing his conception of value in the exertion avoided or saved by the possession of a certain thing, actually encompasses all the different viewpoints mentioned by Pareto: the 'marginal utility', expressed by the desire necessary to induce exertion; the obstacles, that is, the cost of production (although the actual cost of production of a similar thing not the cost of production of the thing itself), and there is labour,

---

56 Henry George: 'The Science of Political Economy'. Robert Schalkenbach Foundation. New York 1981- pages 226-268

not abstract labour but as Marx would say, the "necessary social labour," labour that aims to satisfy some demand, to produce a similar thing now.

But George's analysis goes further, by distinguishing between values from production, those that, being the product of labour, permit the one who purchases the thing to save exertion and toil, and values from obligation, corresponding to those things which are not the product of labour – such as land - but allow the owner to impose toil and exertion to others willing to use it. He surpasses the limits of Paretian analysis and closes the circle of the correct definition of value. This concept of 'value from obligation' is unknown to Pareto, who can find no other solution to the problem posed by things that – like land - having no production cost, does have a value, than to say simply that it is not the 'cost of production' that determines value but the 'whole of the factors of economic equilibrium', that always remain in a certain way undefined.

The Austrian school, starting with Carl Menger, found a solution as well. Menger explained that values are subjective and not inherent in things. That would include products of labour and natural resources not from labour. The prices of consumer goods are determined by the subjective values of the buyers in an auction-like market. The prices of factors, such as land and labour, are then imputed from the prices of the goods they produce. Hence, classical economics has the causation backwards.

Production costs do not determine the prices of goods; rather, the prices of goods determine how much and at what price the factors will be employed. Yes, prices do tend to equal costs of production, but only because if the subjective value of the good is too low, the factors will not be employed at all. If the price of a good yields a high gain in production, more factors will be attracted, increasing the supply, reducing the marginal utility and price, and thus making the price equal to the marginal costs of production. Modern economics adheres to this Austrian explanation of value.

Also alien to Pareto – although he makes of the hedonistic principle the basis of his analysis - is the 'actual' character of the toil, exertion and hardship that determines value, the remarkable concept unveiled by Henry George. Pareto seems to argue as if the factors of economic equilibrium were pre-existent to the determination of value. The concept explained by George, that what determines value is what a similar thing would cost now, was not in Pareto's mind.

For Pareto this 'vague and undetermined thing that the literary economists call value in some relation with prices, depends on all the circumstances, with no exceptions, that influence the determination of economic equilibrium'. Consequently, for Pareto, there is no single cause of value, and thus it is a waste of time to try to find it. For him there are many causes, pre-existent to its determination.

Pareto adds, 'It is good to note that the strength of the opinion according to which there must be one cause for value is so big that even Leon Walras could not avoid it... He (Walras) expresses contradictory notions. On the one hand he says that 'all the unknowns of the economic problem depend on all the equations of economic equilibrium', which is a good theory, and on the other hand he says that it 'is true that marginal utility (ophelimite) is the cause of the value of exchange', and this is reminiscent of past theories that do not correspond with reality. Nevertheless in his texts he points out that the merchandise is 'scarce' for the desires to be satisfied as a consequence of the obstacles that should be faced to obtain it. In this context, that is to say having in mind the obstacles, the notion that 'scarcity is the cause of the value of exchange' is less inaccurate[57].

One can thus summarize that Pareto criticises Walras for giving an explanation of value in contradiction with the logic of his own system. 'For Pareto, Walras disregards the equations of production that are part of general equilibrium since we abandon the narrow picture of theory of interchange. The solution consisting in assigning to the first equations the role of determining the prices of productive services is not correct because the two groups of equations are interdependent: technical progress, modifying production indexes, affects not only the price of productive services, but also the price of products. However, Walras is conscious of this inter-dependence when in his polemic with Ricardo he admits that the price of productive service may have repercussions on the price of the products. This late concession contradicts the thesis of a step by step determination of product and productive services prices: in reality it is the entirety of the equations of the system that determines simultaneously the whole of the unknown, and in this sense Pareto proposes a reading of Walrasian general equilibrium more adequate than Walras

---

57 From 'Manual d'économie politique', Geneve, Droz, 1966 extracted from chapter 3 by Jean Boncoeur and Hervé Thouement 'Histoire des idées economiques – de Walras aux contemporaines' – Nathan- Paris 2000. P. 51 (translated with paraphrasing by Fernando Scornik Gerstein and Fred E. Foldvary).

himself.'[58]

In reality, as much for George as for the marginalists in general, and also for Pareto, value is basically an affection of the human spirit for things, something that belongs to 'me as an individual.'

As George puts it, value is 'a feeling, and so long as it remains merely a feeling, it can be known only to and can be measured only by the one who feels it. It must come out in some way into the objective through action before anyone else can appreciate or in any way measure it... Thus it is that there is no measure of value among men save competition or the haggling of the market, a matter that might be worth the consideration of those amiable reformers who so lightly propose to abolish competition.'[59]

Although George unfortunately lambasts the 'Austrians' with his criticism, it seems to us that at least many of the important marginalists, including Austrians, shared his view on this point. George is attributing to the marginalists something that they don't really say: they do not try to measure subjective feelings. On the contrary, marginal utility, originating value at the margin, the utility of the next item, is the expression in the market of the subjective feelings. George who was acquainted with the works of Jevons, von Wieser, Böhm-Bawerk and Marshall seems not to have understood, or to disregard, the many agreements they had with his own ideas.

    George sometimes includes in 'labour' both the exertion of

---

58 Jean Boncoeur – Hervé Thouement. Ibid p. 52   (translated with paraphrasing by Fernando Scornik Gerstein and Fred E. Foldvary).

59 Henry George. Ibid pages 252-253

a person and the 'obstacles' to overcome; that is, costs such as machinery and raw materials. For George, what determines the cost in relation to value is the whole of the factors operating here and now. It is not only marginal utility, expressing desire, but also the cost of productive services, that is the entirety of the equations of the system (using Pareto's terminology) that determines value, whose sole manifestation can be found in the market.

An economist of the Austrian school would point out here that costs are also subjective, the economic cost being in reality the foregone opportunity, what is given up in doing something. Thus, the opportunity cost of labour is the foregone leisure, and the amount of labour one supplies depends on the relative subjective values, and marginal utilities, of more goods versus more leisure. Land has no opportunity cost, so its market price is unrelated to any social cost, but is based on the marginal utility of extra land or the imputed value of the goods produced at that site.

With this brief view of the basic ideas of Pareto, we can now enter into what we could call the theoretical foundation - to say philosophical might be too much - of Paretian thought, especially on the theory for which his name is famous, Pareto's optimality.

In respect to the fundamentals, like Walras, Pareto analyses that there are two aspects of economics, the pure and the applied. Pure theory is universal and is the first approximation in explaining phenomena such as equilibrium. Pure economic theory for Pareto 'is similar to physical-mathematical sciences: it deals with the essential character and the interdependence the variables in equilibrium in general... Applied economics, on the contrary, should take into account other social sciences, particularly history and sociology'.[60]

He builds his socioeconomic analysis upon what he calls the 'maximum of ophelimite', better known as the 'Pareto optimum'. He starts from the premise that it is impossible to measure interpersonal utility, which cannot be expressed with numbers. Free-trade is based, as stated by Adam Smith, on the idea that the exertions of individuals pursuing their interest and personal benefit, under the pressure of competition, will result in the general welfare of society. This is the famous 'invisible hand' spoken of by Adam Smith. The British philosopher Bentham, founder of philosophical utilitarianism, defined social well being as the sum of the utilities of all the members of society. But the neoclassicals deemed it impossible to compare different persons' satisfactions, as it was impossible to measure an individual's utility.[61]

That is to say, they deemed it impossible to apply the criterion of utilitarian ethics of adding individual utilities to obtain the measure of collective welfare. Such a summing is based on the idea that one could obtain a cardinal numeric value for the utility of an individual.

Pareto affirms that is impossible to do interpersonal comparisons of utility, because each person is the only judge of his satisfaction depending on personal parameters. For Pareto the 'ophelimite' (marginal utility) expresses a relation-

---

60 Baslé, Chavance and others: 'Histoire des Pensées Economiques'. Dalloz. France 1993, p. 187 (translated with paraphrasing by Fernando Scornik Gerstein and Fred E. Foldvary).

61 Op. cit., p. 189 (translated with paraphrasing by Fernando Scornik Gerstein and Fred E. Foldvary).

ship between a person and a thing. This is not some abstract total utility, but something concrete, expressed in the act of consuming the thing. As he says in his 'Cours d'économie politique':

> 'Reduced to the unit of a very small quantity of an economic good added to the quantity we have already enjoyed, this shall be named 'elemental ophelimite', corresponding to that quantity... It is the "final degree of utility" of Jevons; the "marginal utility" of English authors, the "rareté" of Walras; the "grenznutzen" of the German-language [Austrian] authors, the "value of the last atom" of Gossen'.

> Adding the elemental 'ophelimite' of the first portion to that of the second one and so on, we shall have the 'total ophelimite'. [62] Measuring interpersonal utility to obtain 'total ophelimite' will never be a complete even conceptually, because the consumption of one good depends on and is related to the consumption of others.

Pareto proposes a solution to this quandary, based in the 'indifference curves' of the consumer, proposed by F. I. Edgeworth in 1881. He thus develops the theory of 'ordinal utility', based in the assumption that the consumer is capable of classifying in a coherent way different baskets of goods in ordinal orders according to preference. An ' indifference curve' does not represent a cardinal amount of utility, such as a person's height, but just an ensemble of baskets of goods

---

62 Baslé, Chavance and others. Ibid p. 189 (translated with paraphrasing by Fernando Scornik Gerstein and Fred E. Foldvary).

occupying the same level in the preferences of the consumer. The height of the hill of pleasure 'is not measurable. When a consumer passes from one curve to a higher curve, he may say he increases his satisfaction, but not by how much.' In this way the difficulties inherent in the cardinal measure of utility are avoided, but the effectiveness of the system ceases when we try to project comparisons of interpersonal utilities to judge a certain economic condition. 'It is not possible to build by adding elemental functions of collective utility because we are using an ordinal and not a cardinal approach.'[63]

Pareto situates himself on the level of pure economics and at this level he considers it possible to deduce that in a system of perfect competition, prices will be determined in a way to procure for each person coming to the market the maximum of utility. This maximum is impossible to measure and add cardinally since it is based on subjective feelings. But, with ordinal indifference curves, we can determine utility maximization within a budget constraint, namely the highest indifferent curve tangent to the budget line. That tells us the mix of goods that maximizes an individual's utility.

As with this method it is now possible to determine the goods that maximizes an individual's utility, we can now apply this to the economic welfare of a group of persons. Pareto's social optimum consists of reaching such an economic condition, such that it is not possible to improve the position of anyone without worsening that of another. As long as we have not reached this situation, Pareto optimality has not been achieved. A 'Pareto improvement' is then possible, where one can increase the utility of one person without re-

---

63 Baslé, Chavance and others. Ibid. Page 189

ducing that of anyone else. What is distinct in the Paretian approach is that this optimum is a criterion of efficiency rather than of distributive justice.

Pareto efficiency is the criterion that if we have not reached the Pareto optimum, there exists a relative inefficiency, due to the possibility of improving the situation of some without worsening the situation of others. This criterion of efficiency, as pure theory, is independent of the political-economic system. It may be used in a market economy or in a state-collectivist command-economy. Pareto points out that in the case of a collectivist economy, for the system to be 'efficient' would require an omniscient planner, an improbability. But he also points out that in a market economy, perfect competition, i.e. the total absence of pricing power by firms, is something very rarely achieved.

The Paretian criterion is hence a coldly technical method by which to minimally judge the efficiency of an economic system. It can tell us nothing about social justice; Pareto leaves that – in a very Walrasian way – for the applied economics, political science, and sociology.

As stated by Boncoeur and Thouement[64], 'Many efficient states are far less than socially [ethically] optimal, such as a situation in which 9 out of 10 persons can barely live while the tenth lives in opulence. This may well be Pareto-optimal, without being a model of welfare for society'… 'Pareto's theory of utility maximization only states that under particular conditions, including perfect competition, an economy max-

---

64 Jean Boncoeur and Hervé Thouement, Ibid., p. 55 (translated with paraphrasing by Fernando Scornik Gerstein and Fred E. Foldvary).

imizes efficiency. The conditions of the resulting equilibrium depend on the initial distribution of the factors of production: if they are unequally owned, the resulting distribution of the income will most likely be also. The Paretian criterion says nothing about the justice or injustice of an economic system'.

As a consequence, for Pareto the role of economists is to be professionals trained to obtain criteria of efficiency. The function of obtaining greater social justice belongs to political science and to politicians. They are concerned with redistribution, superceding Pareto optimality by giving to one and taking from another.

Nevertheless, Pareto severely criticises all forms of monopoly, because the incomes from them are obtained to the detriment of others. This may perhaps be his only incursion into the field of justice, but for Pareto, it is an incursion necessary to maintain the criteria of economic efficiency.

When he goes into applied economics and enters history and sociology, Pareto's vision is pessimistic. According to him it is useless to try to modify the distribution of income for society as a whole, because the distribution will eventually return to its original condition. As Raymond Aron put it, 'he does not shine any light of hope', and he adds 'If I may say so, the bare facts have very often after half a century proven Pareto right'.[65]

Nevertheless, Pareto's optimality concept was adopted by the theorists of welfare economics, pioneered by Pigou, based precisely on criterions of efficiency that permit improving the situation of society without damaging any sec-

---

65 Cited by Baslé and Chavance, Ibid., p. 196.

tor, a hypothetical ideal with little practical applicability in any system unless it is extended with compensation. That is, for a change in policy, if those who lose utility can be compensated and restored to their previous level, then there can be a Pareto improvement if others are better off even after the compensation.

Thus, for Pareto, a greater equalization of the distribution of wealth seems a goal difficult to reach. According to him it is only possible to improve the standard of living of the poorer classes via economic growth: 'it is necessary that wealth grow faster than population'.[66]

He deduces from the evidence that the distributions of income have remained basically unchanged despite reforms, that this distribution is not a consequence of chance but of human nature. Therefore, the only way to fight against it is with economic growth, which creates more wealth for everyone without a futile interfering with the process of distribution.[67]

Yet in saying this, Pareto, in contrast to some theorists of economic growth, honestly believes that the distribution of wealth has been unjust, even profoundly unjust. He recognises this fact, but declares that we are unable to modify it

---

66 Vilfredo Pareto: 'Cours d'économie politique'. Libraire Droz-Geneve. 1964. Pp. 408-9.

66 Vilfredo Pareto: 'Cours d'économie politique'. Libraire Droz-Geneve. 1964. Pp. 408-9.

67 Analysing the similarity of the distribution of income in different countries, he points out: 'It is absolutely impossible to admit that they are due only to chance. There is certainly a cause that produces the tendency of incomes to draw a certain curve. The shape of this curve has only a weak dependence on the different economic conditions of the countries considered, because the effects are approximately the same for countries where the economic conditions are so different as England, Ireland, Germany... the Italian cities and even Peru (Vilfredo Pareto. Op. cit., p. 312).

due to insurmountable failures in human nature (which he does not specify), and so he forwards economic growth as the only way out. Many modern theorists also propose growth as the only medicine, but conceal, when they don't ignore it, that it is an instrument used precisely to avoid touching a highly unequal distribution of wealth. Some even assert that inequality is beneficial to growth.

Pareto is aware of class struggle and points out that attention should be given to this from the works of Karl Marx and Achille Loria, the latter so unfairly criticized by Frederick Engels[68]. Nevertheless, Pareto is ambivalent with respect to the confrontation of economic classes. On one hand, he points out that if the struggle is done through free markets, it will maximize utility. 'Each class, as each individual, all seeking to satisfy only their personal interest, indirectly benefit all the others'. Furthermore, 'this competition does not diminish the well being of the poor, but rather by the production of wealth, contributes indirectly to improve the level of minimum income and to diminish the inequality of incomes'. [69]

We find here perhaps an ambiguity, because as we have already pointed out, Pareto believes that whatever reforms are introduced, incomes would return to the original curve,

---

68 Achille Loria (1857-1943). Italian economist considered by many one of the greatest supporters of "agrarian socialism". He gave primordial importance in the evolution of societies to the relation between the people and the land. Although he thought that Marxist historic materialism "shows the way" he criticised orthodox Marxism and some of Marx economic thesis. He considered that a change of the social conditions would not come from new dogmas or changes in government, but from a change in property relations. In the foreword to the III rd Volume of "The Capital", Engels answers with insults, to the critics of Loria

69 Vilfredo Pareto. Op. cit., p. 386 (translated with paraphrasing by Fernando Scornik Gerstein and Fred E. Foldvary).

which means that any relative improvement would be only temporary. At any rate, he provides no clarification.

There is yet a greater ambiguity, because on the other hand he adds that there is another type of class struggle: 'that one in which each class tries to seize the government to turn it into a machine of exploitation. The struggle of certain individuals to take possession of the wealth dominates the entire history of humanity. It hides and disappears under the most diverse pretexts, which have often mislead historians... The dominant class does wrong not only to the classes that are dispossessed; it does wrong to the whole nation, because as exploitation generally goes together with the destruction of wealth, often considerable, it reduces the lowest incomes as it increases the inequality in the distribution of income'.[70]

For Pareto it is not really important how this domination is expressed, whether by way of an oligarchy, a plutarchy or a democracy. He only points out that the more numerous the beneficiaries of the system, the more intense the evils, because a large number of privileged people consumes more than a small number.

For this second type of class struggle, Pareto uses a language similar to that of Marx. The difference is that for Marx this is the only type of class struggle, while for Pareto these two struggles can be distinct.

Although he does not give concrete examples, we can infer that for the political class struggle, he thinks of our modern democracies, where class dominance is always there, especially by means of the legal and taxation systems, although other regimes can be worse. There is nevertheless another

---

70 Pareto, Ibid 386-7.

distinction from Marxist thought that may be deduced from the aforesaid.

Pareto in no way believes that in a society of 'popular socialism', as he calls it, things would be better. On the contrary, he thinks that exploitation would be even more terrible, and if we look at what happened in the communist countries, his vision – in 1896- was a far-reaching premonition.[71]

With this summary of the complex and many times ambiguous Paretian thought, we may now analyse and perhaps understand his ideas with respect to territorial property, its importance for society, and the solutions he proposes, always leaving the door open for different hypotheses, as characterizes Pareto's way of reasoning. We shall now enter into the subject of what Pareto calls 'territorial capitals', that is, land and natural resources.

Following Walras' ideas, Pareto differentiates between 'territorial capitals', 'mobile capitals', and 'personal capitals', or in classical terms, land, capital goods, and labour. Pareto uses a terminology akin to the marginalist and the mathematic school in general, which certainly does not contribute to the clarification of the taxonomy of the factors of production. This is the neoclassical attempt, frustrated from the start as we shall see in Pareto's case, to classify land as just another form of capital.

He begins the chapter dedicated to 'territorial capitals' in

---

71 'Inequality in the distribution of income seems to depend more on the human nature itself rather than on the economic organisation of society. Deep modifications of this organization could have but little influence to modify the law of income distribution. Furthermore if mobile and territorial capitals are collective property, the new society will show still a curve of incomes which will be similar –at least in part- to the one we actually observe (Vilfredo Pareto. Ibid. p. 363).

his Applied political economy', by pointing out that economic theory should take territorial capitals in 'the condition they are', that is to say, without differentiating the improvements made in the past that are incorporated into earth: fertilizers, canals, drainage of swamps, etc., for which it would be difficult to distinguish the improvement value from that of the land free of improvement, a criterion put forth also by Henry George, and which in any case matches a pragmatic vision.

He then presents a thesis which is apparently basic for him:

> 'The price of the services of territorial capitals is established, at least as a first approximation, in the same way as the price of the services of all the other capitals, namely, the price that equalizes the quantities supplied and demanded.' [72]

However, he immediately points out that when it comes to the investment of savings in new capitals, there are substantial differences. While savings can be applied to mobile capitals (steam engines, ships, houses) and to personal capitals (what is now called human capital: skills, training education), in contrast 'there are other capitals for which savings can be transformed only with great difficulty: those capitals for which the quantity remains fixed, given a closed economy. Those are territorial capitals, mines, etc.' [73]

He indicates, as a consequence, that the possessors of natural resources are in a better position than the others to secure extraordinary benefits in the case of increasing demand; while the other capitals, in the same case of increasing demand for their services, can only secure benefits for more or

72 Pareto, Ibid., p. 391.

73 Pareto, Ibid p. 392.

less short periods, because attracted by the high profits, new capitals will come and the competition will tend to reduce the price and profits. In contrast, the holders of territorial capitals 'enjoy a more concrete monopoly, which in certain cases can be an absolute one. They will be able to obtain substantial gains.'[74]

Although he states that while the open-economy possibility of trade in natural resources should be considered, he indicates that due to the fixed and untransferable character of spatial land, this can only be done through the services or the products acquired with those services.

Thus the first observation of Pareto that the price of the services of territorial capitals (the rent) is fixed in the same way as the prices of the services of all the other capitals may now be seen to have significant qualifications. The rent of land is determined in the same way as the return to other factors only with respect to the economic process, the elements of supply and demand, but the essence is different because 'territorial capitals' are different. The effect on society and the implications for policy are profoundly different between land and the other factors.

As Pareto himself points out, land is immobile and fixed in its amount within some territorial boundary. As a consequence, rent is a monopoly price, in the classical sense of monopoly as an industry in which there is no entry to expand supply. Capital goods do not generally have such a monopoly, since a higher return attracts firms to increase the supply. What for land is the rule, monopoly, is for mobile capitals the exception although in modern scale economies

---

74 Pareto, Ibid., p. 392 .

there are monopolic and oligopolic situations that can embrace long periods.

We see here the confusion that can come from using the term 'territorial capital' for something that is not a capital good.

In addition, Pareto says that

'the economic importance of territorial capitals
has been exaggerated up to the point of pretending
that the principal cause of poverty is the fact that
all lands are occupied.' [75]

If they were not, if there were free land, the capitalist would not be able to appropriate a surplus value because the worker instead of being employed by the capitalist, 'could establish himself on a plot on free land'.

Pareto criticises this theory, indicating that there is a lack of capitals and not of land, although further on he clarifies that it is not so in old countries where there is lack of land and not of capitals. Besides, he indicates that even if there may be free land in new countries, the person wanting a certain site, for example in Paris, will not accept a plot in the Pampas. He adds another alleged error, 'consisting in thinking that any man could be a farmer'.

Pareto's reasoning ends here, leaving everything in twilight. In developed countries there is no free land, in the 'new' countries there is, but this is often not relevant, and although it is quite clear that not everyone can be a farmer, what Pareto does not say is that no supporter of geoclassical theory, that such as of Walras and George regarding land,

---

75 Pareto, op. cit., p. 394 .

proposes any such thing. Were there to be additional lands in the local economy, free of rent, of the productive quality already existing, it would increase the marginal product of labour, and thus the wage level, since that portion of output now going to rent would instead go to wages.

After this rather confused, indeed unlearned, cogitation, Pareto reaches a conclusion even more surprising:

> 'But if the economic importance of territorial property has been exaggerated, its social importance remains intact. In our societies, from ancient times until nowadays, political power has belonged, with rare exception, to the owners of the land... and there must be some reason to explain the privileges which the possessors of territorial capitals enjoy'.[76]

We could question ourselves how it is possible that something with 'little economic importance' has such a great social importance and be the base of so much political power. Clearly, it makes no sense. It is obvious that the one thing is related to the other. It is the economic importance that generates the special importance and the political power!

In spite of the evidence, Pareto, already in an ocean of confusion and contradictions,[77] deems it necessary to investigate 'if those privileges are or are not separable from the possession of territorial capitals'. 'If we may separate them, he con-

---

76 Pareto, Ibid., pp. 396-7.

77 Pareto criticises Achilles Loria stating that in spite of the fact that he has brought light into these problems, he commits according to Pareto 'the mistake of confounding the use of territorial capitals with the abuse that may come together with them', a very peculiar criticism coming from an economist like Pareto who makes of individual egoism one of the basis of his economic construction.

tinues, we may consider territorial capitals exclusively from the economic point of view, and the maximum of utility will be obtained by the free market... If on the contrary we are able to demonstrate that ownership of territorial property is, at least in our societies, totally linked with the faculty of extracting contributions from the rest of the population, the problem would change completely and we could not then separate the economic from the social part[78].'

If the latter be true, Pareto suggests various solutions, which he mentions one by one, but at the end opts for none. At any rate, the solutions are for a problem whose existence is not clear for him.

The first solution is really pyrrhic: to simply accept the privileged situation that territorial property gives to certain citizens. For Pareto there is nothing in that notion which is contrary to general utility.

A second 'solution' would be to extend property rights in land to almost every citizen, in which case, he says, it would cease to be a privilege. This was the position of the Catholic Church and what has been achieved in developed countries as Spain and others and to a small degree been attempted in some developing countries. We may see not only that it is not a solution, but also that it makes it more difficult to come to the effective one. Pareto forgets the new generations, the constant increase in population, that creates ever more dispossessed. At any rate, Pareto does not really like this solution, because 'nations in which a large part of the population

78 Pareto, Ibid., p. 397.

are small owners do not have exceptionally notable moral and political qualities'. Besides, he says, small property reconciles itself with difficulty with large industry (he seems to refer to agriculture).

Hence he comes to the third solution, the socialist one of 'giving to the state the property of territorial capitals and moreover, generally, also the property of mobile capitals, conferring to it at the same time the indirect advantages that are joined to these properties". [79] He does not analyse, until further on, the possibility of nationalizing only land, and when he does, it is more as an option for new countries.

Pareto takes pains to reject the socialist solution, saying that there is no guarantee that the destruction of wealth would be less in such a system, although he accepts that if all capitals would be transformed into collective property the land rent would benefit the entire society instead of only enriching some individuals. He equates the collective property of all capitals with the theory that proposes that each worker would be the owner of the territorial and mobile capitals he uses, which he considers an impossible achievement in practice.

Further, he enters into a rather confused discussion on the Socialist State which, besides collecting rents, would also collect taxes to create new capitals, a thing that we know is one of the few mistakes that communism – as a general rule – did not commit. It was not necessary since by fixing prices and salaries, the state kept the lion's share.

As for compensating the owner in the case of the purchase of land by the state, Pareto is again ambiguous, stating that

---

79 Pareto, ibid., p. 397.

there are no reasons to be in favour or against it, as it will depend on the time and country, since, according to him, it is impossible to know in advance if it will benefit the state due, to the variations in land prices, "although the general movement is upwards". [80]He does not even mention the proposals of Gossen and Walras, which demonstrate the benefit that nationalization would give to the state, even after paying compensation to the owners.

Regarding new countries, he leaves open for the government to decide which is more convenient, the option to lease land for long periods (100 years) or to sell it,. The possibility of leasing the land for shorter or even longer periods but with a periodically revised assessment [81]is not even discussed by him, which makes obvious the lack of thoroughness with which he looked to the problem of rent.

Pareto is not inclined to any of the described solutions, except perhaps to the Georgist one, although he does not attribute this to George, but in partial error to John Stuart Mill and in total error to Leon Walras, who favoured the nationalization of land.

When he deals with the Ricardian concept of rent, Pareto states, "J. S. Mill saw in the increase of the rent ... a taxable object. This would be, in any case, a better solution that the

---

80 Pareto, Ibid. P. 400.

81 The first Argentinean president, Bernardino Rivadavia, passed in 1826 a "Law of Emphiteusis" in virtue of which land was leased for periods of 20 years with an annual rent of 8% of the value for the first 10 years on land dedicated to cattle breeding and of 4% on land dedicated to agriculture. Land values would be determined by a Jury of neighbours, and every 10 years land values should be re-assessed and the rent updated. The law was repeal by the Argentinean parliament in 1857. General Bartolomé Mitre, a national hero, said it was a "communist law". We all know what happened afterwards in Argentina.

one we first examined (the socialist one) within an exclusively theoretical goal. Walras also deals with this questions."[82]

We know that John Stuart Mill's proposal was to tax the unearned increments on land values, something similar to our capital gains tax but applied only to the value of land, but he did not put forward a general system of land taxation. As to Leon Walras it is not that he "also deals with these questions", but dedicates to them a substantial part of his works, and he does not propose a tax but the repurchase of land from the owners as the way to make land rent the main source of revenue for the State, suppressing all other taxes, as we have discussed in detail above.

In spite of his general pessimism and failure to give due thorough analysis to land , Pareto seems to have seen in the taxation of rent a possible solution, at least theoretically.

The essence of Pareto is his relativism and his pessimism. Relativism, because he thinks that optimal types of land tenure may vary according to the country, the historical moment of its development and the economic conditions. Times have not always been as they are now, and for sure they will change in the future, and regarding which is the best system "we have unfortunately very little light on the matter. We only know for certain that types of property and of land exploitation must vary according to the circumstances.[83] It is possible that there is not only one evolution of territorial property, but many, that may differ according to peoples and places. We should study them separately without pre-conceptions,

---

82 Pareto, ibid. Note in p. 127, parag. 783, of Volume II.

83 Pareto, Ibid., p. 410.

observing the facts of the present and obtaining historical documents for the past".[84]

Pessimism, because based on the above discussed permanence of income distribution curves, he affirms: "if men do not become better, the shape of the social regime may change, but not its substance".[85]

Nevertheless within his pessimism it seems clear that, in the end, Pareto is inclined to a system of free trade, with private ownership of capitals – which would secure a maximum of social utility – as long as somehow, maybe through taxation - the weighty problem of land rent is tackled and a permanent fight is carried out against the structures safe-guarding monopolies, basically protectionism and state intervention in favour of certain capitals, mainly the territorial ones. He points out that when the rent of land is the consequence of "acts of government", it would be sufficient to impede those acts for it to disappear. With this statements he is showing to us that the effect of social progress on rent – which generally consists of increasing it - is something he did not really understand. Following the logic of his thoughts all acts of good government should be stopped, because almost every action of good government tends to increase the rent!

To really understand the failures, doubts and contradictions in the paretian analysis of "territorial capitals" we must analyse what we deem to be also his failures and ambiguities in his analysis of the rent of land.

He starts by criticizing the definition of rent given by Ri-

---

84 Pareto, Ibid., p. 416.

85 Pareto, ibid., p. 394.

cardo: "rent, says Ricardo, is that part of the product of land paid to the owner for the right to exploit the natural and indestructible faculties of the ground". According to Pareto this definition has no meaning at all, because every time that a person acquires a service, he acquires the right to exploit "natural faculties". In the breeding of rabbits, for example, there is the faculty of reproduction that nature gives to rabbits, or when we pay the visit of a doctor, we acquire, at least partly, the use of the natural faculties of his brain. "There is a part which is radically false in Ricardo's theory, and is based on the wrong principle that value is the product of labour. As it happens that after having formulated the principle we must face cases in which goods have value without any relation to human labour, he thought he could overcome this obstacle by imagining that we are paying "the work of natural agents" and hence the name of "increment" given to the rent, to indicate that it has not been earned by the labour of the owner.[86]

Really, the error is Pareto's. It is correct that Ricardo gave that definition, but it suffices to read all that he says after that in Chapter II of his "Principles" to understand that in his conception, the origin of rent is not from "natural agents," which Ricardo recognizes as existing also in industry, but the fixed character of land.

If there were an abundance of free land, affirms Ricardo, "following the common principles of supply and demand, no rent would be paid for that land, for the same reasons that nothing is paid for air and water or for any of the gifts of nature which exist in unlimited quantity. With a given quantity of materials and with the assistance of atmospheric pressure

---

86 Pareto, Ibid. Volume II. P. 113, parag 758.

and steam elasticity, machines may do their jobs and abbreviate human labour greatly, but no charge is demanded for the use of these natural aids, because they are inexhaustible and at the disposal of any person... It is only then because land is not unlimited in quantity and uniform in quality and that due to progress in population, land of inferior quality or less well located is called to culture, that a rent is paid for its use"[87]

Hence, it is not the "natural faculties" as such, but the monopolistic character they have in connection with land, which originates rent. That is why there is always rent, even under a socialist regime. Private ownership of land only permits appropriation of the rent by the land owner.

Regarding value as the product of labour, what Ricardo said, quoting Adam Smith, is that the true price of everything, what it really costs to the person willing to acquire it, is the 'toil and difficulties to obtain it'.

'What anything is really worth for the man who has acquired it and now wishes to dispose of it or exchange it for another thing, is the toil and difficulties he may save and impose on other persons'.[88] Implicitly, this recognizes that the true economic cost of labour is the opportunity loss, the foregone leisure, and this is the ultimate cost, as land has for society no economic cost. However, as an explanation of value, the Austrians are clearer in tracing all market prices to subjective values.

87 David Ricardo: "The Principles of Political Economy and Taxation"- The Guernsly Press Co. Ltd. London 1992, pages 34/35

88 Ricardo, Ibid., p. 6 (translated with paraphrasing by Fernando Scornik Gerstein and Fred E. Foldvary).

In spite of this, and after the attack, Pareto ends by saying that the results obtained by Ricardo are acceptable, at least partly: further on – now in full contradiction - Pareto affirms that the price paid for the use of land "does not differ at all from that paid for the use of any other capital, for example, a machine", adding that what makes the difference between land and the machine is that savings can be easily transformed into new machines, while generally it is not possible to transform them into new lands.[89]

Pareto criticizes also, without solid basis, the Ricardian concept that rent is not a part of the cost of production. (Ricardo's famous statement is, corn is not high because rent is high; rather, rent is high because the price of corn is high.) Pareto analyses this in an unsystematic way, sometimes from the point of view of an economist observing the facts and for whom the rent is not a part of the cost, and other times from the position of the firm for which rent is undoubtedly a part of its cost.

Pareto continues by putting forward some questions to be answered:

- Does rent exist for all territorial capitals or only for some of them?
- Is rent something special referring only to territorial capitals?
- What is the origin of rent?
- Is rent useful for mankind or for a particular society?
- Are there means to remedy the evils caused by rent without producing even greater evils?

---

89 Pareto, Ibid., Vol. II, p. 114, parag. 759.

Pareto's answer to the first question is that rent exists for almost all land. The more accurate answer is that rent exists for land whose productivity is greater or equal to that at the margin of production, beyond which submarginal land has no market rent.

With respect to the second one the answer is negative. For Pareto rent is not exclusive of territorial capitals, as other capitals in specific circumstances may produce rents, although land rent is the most important.[90]

With reference to the origin of rent he says that "it is due to the cause of all values, that is to say to the marginal utility of the services of the capital. In particular, it is due to the differences in productivity among such capitals, related to the fluency with which we may obtain them by saving.[91]

With respect to (4) the "usefulness of the rent for mankind or for a particular society," his answer is negative:

"economically rent diminishes the marginal utility enjoyed by society, because it creates obstacles to the equality of the net rates of interest, which is a condition for the maximum of marginal utility".[92]

We can note here that if almost all the rent is collected for public revenue, then land is not purchased for its return, and the rent no longer negatively affects the rate of interest.

For the last question, we have an extraordinary and precise observation, totally coinciding with the viewpoints of Walras and George: rent is the price of a monopoly affecting

90 Pareto, Ibid., p. 124.

91 Pareto Ibid. p. 124.

92 Pareto, Ibid., p. 128.

the whole society and creating, when private appropriation is allowed, a sector of privileged people, and causing economic distortions! Pareto is clear about the fact that the rent is a tax paid by the rest of society to territorial proprietors; however, he thinks that the methods proposed to abolish this appropriation of rent could be even more harmful for society.

Pareto accepts the validity of Henry George's criticism of "territorial property in the United States", introducing in this way a geographic limit which really does not match with George ideas, since as we know his ideas do not refer to one country, but to private appropriation of rent in general.

In connection with the remedies, Pareto is rather obscure. He seems to believe that in a right of property always scrupulously respected, "the advantages for society would surpass the inconveniences that it may produce", [93]although it is difficult to understand what he really means. Either there is private appropriation of rent or there is not. If there is, evils are unavoidable, they are inherent to the system, they do not depend on the goodness or evilness of the landowners.

Nationalization of land seems to him a remedy worse than the sickness, although he points out that the main problem in connection with rent resides in the fact that is not uniform in space and time and hence it is difficult to reach a satisfactory general solution.

However his position is clear in the sense of fighting against speculation and against government policies that tend to increase rent artificially. Although he is far from being clear, Pareto seems inclined, as we have explained, to solutions based on taxation, at least for appreciation.

---

93 Pareto, Ibid., p. 128.

Although we may blame Pareto for being ambiguous and sometimes contradictory in this subject, we may with good textual evidence conclude, despite his denials, a recognition by Pareto of the distinctive character of land as an economic factor.

VI. Conclusion

In this paper we wish to widen the understanding on the ideas of these four marginalists, and to have shown that, with shadings and great differences in degree, the subject of land and natural resources was very especially analyzed by them, having in some cases, especially with Walras, a central and immovable place in theory and policy.

Much has been written on Henry George and the marginalists, about their coincidences, remarkable at times, and about the differences that set them apart. In this sense the essay by Leland Yeager seems excellent to us.[94]

Doubtless, George had many more things in common with the marginalists than he thought he had, and vice versa. It is not the intention of this paper to analyze them, but we should point out that, in general, when both schools of thought – the Georgist and the marginalist - have been under scrutiny, the analysis has often not focused on the land issue, although

---

94 Leland B Yeager: "Henry George and Austrian Economics" in George and the Scholars. Robert Schalkenbach Foundation. New York 1991. Pp. 191-208.

there have been exceptions.[95]

Many scholars have taken for granted that for the marginalist, land is simply a form of capital. We believe we have shown that for some of the most distinguished, this was not so. For these – Gossen, von Wiesar, and Walras – the determination of the price of land and other factors coincide in method, but do not coincide in the economic impact the and in the characteristics of the object of valuation.

Regarding the unfortunately derogatory attitude of George toward the marginalists, we believe it may have a simple explanation: George had discovered and gained an understanding of a great social truth. He was not the first to see it, but was the first one to express it as a central moral and economic concept, doing so with pristine clarity and impeccable logic to the public. For the thinker that has before his eyes a truth of this kind, the supposed experts that do not see this deserve to be chastised. If marginal analysis shunts land to the margins, then something must be very wrong with the analysis. Had he known the works of Gossen and Walras, maybe he would have changed his attitude.

Finally, some thoughts about Pareto's "pessimism". We believe due attention should be paid to his words. It is not an unbased idea: the historical curves of distribution of income are there. However, the distribution of income varies widely among countries, and notably, in Taiwan during the last half of the 20th century its economy achieved a high rate of growth with a remarkably egalitarian distribution of income,

---

95 In this sense, is interesting the study of Renato Cirillo: 'Economists and Social Reformers on Land Ownership and Economic Rent' in 'George and the Scholars'. Ibid. pp. . 209-224.

and without welfare-statist redistribution. No doubt its land reform and the taxation of land in the early stages of its development after 1950 contributed to both the growth and equality. Pareto's pessimism applies when reforms only treat the effects of inequality, but not, evidently, when the causes are confronted and remedied.

One of the present authors has pointed out in another book [96]that the hedonistic principle moulds human conduct and social institutions. In it psychological version which holds that human actions are motivated primarily by a search for pleasure and the avoidance of pain and as a consequence in the obtention of the maximum benefit with the least exertion, it is the central principle of human behavior and thus of economic analysis. If the hedonist principle is not controlled, if we are not vigilant about its effects in the social order, it will be as difficult to put an end to private appropriation of rent, as it was to end slavery.

Both are institutions at the service of human egoism and based in the law of "the maximum benefit with the less exertion", and as such are extremely difficult to combat.

However, we must persevere. After thousands of years of accepting it, slavery is now universally condemned.

As Victor Hugo said: "there is nothing in the world more powerful than an idea for which the time has come". Sooner or later, the time will come for those who believe that land, the physical space in which we live, is the common heritage of Humanity.

---

96 Fernando Scornik Gerstein: "The Future of Taxation". The Blakesley Press in association with the Centre for Land Policy Studies. London 1999. Part IV-23- "The Hedonistic Principle".

The Marginalists

Bibliography

B

Baslé, Chavance and others: "Historie des Pensées Economiques" – Dalloz – France 1993.

Böhm – Bawerk, Eugen: "Fundamentos de la Teoría del Valor de los Bienes Económicos" - Leningrad1929.

Böhm-Bawerk, Eugen: "Of Capital and Interest" – Libertarian Press, South Holland, Illinois, 1959

Boncour, Jean and Thouement, Hervé: "Histoire des idées économiques" – Nathan, Paris 2000.

C

Cirillo, Renato: "Economists and Social Reformers on Land Ownership and Economic Rent, in "George and the Scholars" – Robert Schalkenbach Foundation, New York 1991.

E

Ekelund, Robert B and Hébert, Robert F: "Historia de la Teoría Económica y de su Método – Mc GrawHill International en España, S.A, - Madrid 1922

G

Gaffney, Mason and Harrison, Fred: "The Corruption of Economics" – Shepheard – Walwyn – London 1994

George, Henry: "The Science of Polital Economy" – The Robert Schalkenbach Foundation, New York 1981.

George, Henry: "Progress and Poverty" – The Robert Schalkenbach Foundation, New

York, 1975

George, Henry: "Protectionism or Free Trade" – The Robert Schalkenbach Foundation, New York, 1992

Gossen, Hermann Heinrich: "The Rules of Human Relations and the Rules of Human Actions Derived Therefrom" – Mit Press, Cambridge, Massachussets, USA, 1983.

H
Harrison Fred: "The Power in the Land". Shepheard – Walwyn Ltd. London 1983

K
Katariev, N. Rindina, M.: "Historia de las Doctrinas Económicas – Editorial Cartago – Buenos Aires 1965

M
Marx, Karl: "El Capital", Fondo de Cultura Económica, México, 1946

Marx, Karl Engels, Friedrich: "The Comunist Manifesto", Oxford University Press, New York, 1992

P
Pareto, Vilfredo: "Cours d'Economie Politique" – Librairie Droz, Geneve 1964

Pareto, Vilfredo: "Manual d'Economie Politique" – Librairie Droz, Geneve 1966.

R
Ricardo, David: "The Principles of Political Economy and Taxation" – The Guernsly Press Co. Ltd. London 1992.

S
Scornik Gerstein, Fernando: "Argentina, in "Land Value Taxation around the World" – The American Journal of Economics and Sociology, Blackwell Publishers, MA, USA, 2000.

Scornik Gerstein, Fernando: "The Future of Taxation" – The Blakesley Press. London 1999.

Silagi, Michael: "Henry George and Europe" – The Robert Schalkenbach Foundation, New York, 2000.

V
Von Mises, Ludwig: "La Acción Humana" – Unión Editorial S.A., Madrid 1986

Von Wieser, Friedrich: "Der Naturliche Wert" – Viena, 1914.

W

Walras, León: "Etudes
d'Economie Sociale" in "Oeuvres économiques complétes"
of August and León Walras –
Paris Economica 1990.

Y
Yeager, Leland B: "Henry
George and Austrian Econom-
ics" in "George and the Schol-
ars" – The Robert Shalkenbach
Foundation – New York 1991

Notes

The Austrians:
Von Mises; Menger; Hayek

Notes

Fernando Scornik Gerstein

Fernando Scornik Gerstein was born and educated in Argentina, where he graduated as a lawyer in 1963. Specializing in agrarian and taxation law, he was legal Advisor to the Argentinean Agrarian Cooperatives for 10 years. Later he was appointed Advisor on Land Taxation to the Minister of Economy and subsequently to the Secretary of State of Agriculture for whom he produced a report – The Basis for a Tax System on the Rent of Land – which was published in 1973. He chaired, in 1975, the Special Commission on the Taxation of Land's Potential Rent set up by the Secretary of State for Agriculture. Being politically active and sensing the dramatics events that were to unfold, he left Argentina for Spain in 1976, where he pursued his legal career. He is the President of AEPERS (Asociación Española para el Estudio del Regimen del Suelo y los Recursos Naturales) and also of the International Union for Land Taxation and Free Trade.

His other published books include:

"Francia: legislación agraria", *"El Impuesto a la Tierra"*, *"Desalojos Rurales"*, *"Bases para un regimen impositivo sobre la renta del suelo"*, *"Tenencia de la Tierra para una Sociedad más Justa"* (all published in Argentina).

"Poll Tax; the Tax that Sank a Government" and *"The Future of Taxation"* (published in the United Kingdom).

Fred E. Foldvary

Fred E. Foldvary teaches economics at Santa Clara University, California. His Ph.D. in economics is from George Mason University. His books include Soul of Liberty, Beyond Neoclassical Economics, Public Goods and Private Communities, Dictionary of Free Market Economics, and (co-edited) The Half-Life of Policy Rationales. Foldvary is also a director of the Civil Society Institute at Santa Clara University, an associate editor of the online journal Econ Journal Watch, and serves on the editorial board of the American Journal of Economics and Sociology. He also writes a weekly column for the online journal www.progress.org.

His main areas of research and articles include public economics, social ethics, real estate economics, and private communities.

www.foldvary.net / ffoldvary@scu.edu

Lightning Source UK Ltd.
Milton Keynes UK
07 July 2010
156668UK00001B/81/P